the

illuminated

BRAND

BUILDING A CULTURE THAT REMAINS

BRANDCENTRIC EVEN UNDER PRESSURE

Two Time Best Selling
Wall Street Journal Author

DAVID M. CORBIN

The Illuminated Brand
Building a Culture that Remains Brandcentric
Even Under Pressure

David M. Corbin
Copyright © 2021
Sigma Press

ISBN: 978-0-578-96934-3

Printed in the United States of America

To my beloved wife, Anne Marie Smith,
whose light and love fill me up every single day,
literally since the moment we met.

acknowledgements

*"The greatest thing you'll ever learn is just to love…
and be loved in return."*
Nat King Cole

I hereby acknowledge these folks for the love I feel for them and the love I've received from them. Yep, "love is all there is."

My family is an enormous source of joy and inspiration in my life: my daughter, Jenna; son, Ben; their spouses (my bonus children), Lila and Guy; and my grandchildren, Libby, Eitan, and Aya, all whom I've been only able to see virtually because of our pandemic, but whom I hope to hold and love up close asap.

What a jolt of energy I experienced when, at lunch, discussing the creation of this book, Mitch Axelrod suggested the term *Involuntary BrandSlaughter*, the perfect moniker for an important part of this book. Building on the title of my previous book, *Preventing BrandSlaughter*, this book deals with the topic of preventing brandslaughter during situations that are done "unto you and upon you," hence the term *Involuntary BrandSlaughter*. Brilliant wordsmithing to capture the point. Thanks, Mitch. (Oh, and I reciprocated that gift with this one: After Mitch suffered a terrible stroke, they discovered a brain tumor, which, if undetected, may well have killed him. They operated, Mitch was a courageous champion and thank goodness he's doing very well. My idea for his next book title? A Stroke of Luck!)

More often than not, books are *conceived* of by authors but actually *written* by professional writers often know as ghost writers. Let me identify the ghost—one who rarely appears on the front of the book but is the genius wordsmith in bringing this message out. Patti McKenna is my ghost. She's worked on most of my books, and I celebrate her for her magnificent writing on this one. She's been such a gift to me in expressing the concepts that I feel so strongly about, those that I've personally used and help others apply to make and sustain positive change. Thanks, Patti, so much. (She will have edited every single word in this book, except *this* paragraph!)

Kerry Jacobson is responsible for the marketing of books that culminate in their reaching bestseller status on *Wall Street Journal*, *USA Today*, *New York Times*, and others. Books need to be worthy to achieve this status, but good books still need the marketing push to get influencers to read and share the good news. Kerry is masterful at that, and I appreciate his successful efforts in doing this with some of my books and achieving WSJ bestseller status.

I am inspired by many of my colleagues who have contributed to my thinking, my happiness, and my success—colleagues like Rob Angel, inventor of Pictionary, Dr. Greg Reid, founder of Secret Knock, the world-famous business event, UGG Boot founder Brian Smith, brand builder extraordinaire and wonderful speaker/author, Mitch Axelrod, mentioned above is my one-man mastermind and lifelong friend. His books are profound, especially *Soul, Role, Goal.*

Rob, Greg, Brian, Mitch, you've blessed me beyond words.

Sharon Lechter, author of *Think and Grow Rich for Women* and also the co-author of *Rich Dad, Poor Dad,* is my dear friend and mentor in so many ways, especially in living gracefully and with poise. Sharon is the epitome of smart meets nice meets generosity.

Steve Farber is one of my favorite writers and thought leaders, and just "settin'" on my back porch, we contemplate lofty ideas and dumb jokes. Seriously, though, folks, Steve's LEAP model from his *Extreme Leader* book has changed the way I see the art of leadership. And his mantra and book, *LOVE is Just Damn Good Business,* reminds me of and confirms my deepest knowing: love is all ya need.

My early mentor and business partner, Brian Tracy, has influenced just about every aspect of my business career. The most encyclopedic mind I've ever encountered, Brian integrates multiple disciplines in the most unique, cogent, and useful manner, and rarely a day goes by that I don't access one of his teachings.

Frank Shankwitz, 1948-2021, founder of Make-A-Wish Foundation, was a great friend. Oh, how we argued … with love and respect. His contributions to my personal expansion were many. He taught us all that through contribution "everyone can be a hero." His life is covered in the film, *Wishman*. I highly recommend it.

Dave Meltzer, Michael Drew, Berny Dohrmann (RIP), my pickleball brothers, Ron, Rich, and Jonny; my tennis brother, Joey, Seid, Richard, Maria and Ray Speth, Wendy Darling, Tony Alessandra, Phil Wexler … thank you for your gifts.

Many thanks to David Getoff, our Naturopath and Board Certified Nutritionist. Why? Because David is a brilliant, gifted mentor in the area of healthy living. He reads and works from blood panels like no other. He works with the infinite wisdom of the body to determine the nutrients needed for supplementation, and he has more life "hacks" than anyone I know. He helps us maintain vibrant health with all of this, and without it we might fall into the abyss of that SAD Standard American Diet and depart before our "expiration date."

And my protégés—those many wonderful beings whom I've had the privilege of mentoring over my career, I acknowledge you. I've taught, spewed whatever wisdom I mustered, introduced you to my friends and colleagues, and also learned so much from you. There are too many to mention by name, but you know who you are. I've watched you learn and grow and create magnificence in and through your lives. Thank you for being on the path to greatness. We need you; we love you.

Finally, I acknowledge you, dear reader, and the readers of my other books. My soul food is hearing that you've taken some of my shared ideas and put them to work, created results, and contribute to yourself and others. Really, it fortifies me as much as the vitamins and supplements from my naturopath.

I ask that you share these stories with me by sending an email to me at david@davidcorbin.com and feed my soul!

people are talking about
THE ILLUMINATED BRAND...

The Illuminated Brand is destined to be yet another one of David's best sellers. David knows just how to engage his readers and his clients to get the message across in a story that will touch and inspire. Through illuminating the potential worst-case scenarios, you can *face it, follow it, fix it* and come out on top.

Dr. Steven Ross Co-Founder,
Chief Clinical & Education Officer CYGENEX

David's newest book, *The Illuminated Brand*, blends his previous two books into easy-to understand lessons that the fictional Reliant Hospital discovers - lessons that you'll want to adapt into your business ASAP. Any of your employees can destroy your hard-earned brand reputation in one dumb move. It happens. But in *The Illuminated Brand*, you see solid strategies to put to use immediately that get all of your people aligned with your brand values so that they know how to "carry the brand" in every interaction they have.

Dr. Tony Alessandra, author of *The Platinum Rule®*
and *The NEW Art of Managing People*

When Dave told me his vision for *The Illuminated Brand,* I had a light bulb moment. I said, "This is the antidote for a deadly new strain of business virus ... *Involuntary BrandSlaughter*! The brand asset is decreasing in value. They have to face it, follow it and fix it." According to Churchill, "Courage is the quality that guarantees all the others." MLK said about integrity, "The time is always right to do what's right." Dave says you're either green and growing or ripe and rotting. So, too, is your brand. In *The Illuminated Brand,* you experience what happens when courage is combined with integrity and powered by doing what's right. In simple terms, Dave lays out the exact blueprint for you to prevent *BrandSlaughter* and become The Illuminated Brand™.

Read this book now. You'll be sorry if your competitors get their hands on it first. Then hire Dave because you'll be REALLY sorry if they get to him first.

Mitch Axelrod, #1 Best Selling Author, The NEW Game of Business™ and The NEW Game of Selling™

David Corbin's latest book, *The Illuminated Brand,* is a treasure trove of great advice for today's business folks trying to navigate the incredibly complex environment we are in now, which then leads to a future choked with uncertainty. By following the advice the book provides and building brand integrity, today's leaders take a big step in navigating this transitional period. The business world is changing for good, and David's book makes it a little less scary.

Larry Namer, Founder E! Entertainment, Chairman LJN Media

Once you have a brand of a product or service, you will need help in letting others know—by sharing, marketing, and living that brand. Read best-selling author David Corbin's newest book, *The Illuminated Brand,* because it will provide the path for you to follow and succeed. I'm a fan.

Don Green, Executive Director, Napoleon Hill Foundation

I am a big fan of my dear friend David Corbin's best-selling books, *Illuminate* and *Preventing BrandSlaughter.* His new book, *The Illuminated Brand,* is an easy-to-understand system that identifies issues with brand contact points to see where the brand is out of integrity and, at the same time, shows how to set strategic brand initiatives, maintain brand alignment, create a brand-centric culture with all stakeholders and build your brand value. Great read, great lessons.

Alec Stern, 8-time Co-Founder including Constant Contact, Founding Team Member "America's Startup Success Expert" AlecSpeaks.com

We don't always equate an organization's brand with employee engagement. However, each and every employee is either enhancing their organization's brand or putting it at risk. David Corbin illuminates the critical components of identifying the organization's weaknesses, while also discovering and utilizing previously hidden strengths. When following this approach, your organization is best positioned for success.

Wendy Darling, GTD Consulting
www.gothedistanceconsulting.com
Miraculous Living Institute www.wendydarling.com

My favorite part of *The Illuminated Brand* is that it focuses on one of the universal truths: if you choose to be honest and vulnerable about your brand, you truly become invulnerable.

Dave Meltzer, host The 2 Minute Drill television show

Integrity is the foundation on which a great brand is built. This book not only shows you how to build a solid brand foundation, but also how to get your team to live the brand in that same level of integrity upon which it was built.

Dave Austin, international bestselling co-author of *Be a Beast: Unleash Your Animal Instincts for Performance Driven Results*

Don't just read this story ... devour the lessons that Reliant Hospital discovers—lessons that you'll want to adapt stat. You'll recognize some of the archetypal fictional characters because you've confronted them in your career. Learn how they engage all stakeholders, even the naysayers, into the total brand mission. It's amazing and very practical to implement. No wonder so many people have endorsed *The Illuminated Brand* book and training program.

Gary Blair, The Goals Guy, 100-Day Challenge

The book that serves as a "wrap-up" on strategy, *The Illuminated Brand* took me back to long hours of strategic planning and many years of changes in existing plans, but not enough results. I wish I had this book in my hands when I was trying to "illuminate" my plans, my visions, and my strategies from my days of nursing in the NYC Health System, to my days of leading 10,000 men and women in the National Guard. It is a must have, must read, and must implement.

Marta Carcana, Brigadier General Retired US Army

I wish David Corbin would have written this book 20 years ago. The concept of brand integrity he shares in this highly engaging story would have helped the hospitals we've worked with to better understand the importance of building a culture of ownership where employees at every level are committed stakeholders for the organization's brand identity. Especially in the post-pandemic world, where every healthcare organization faces staffing challenges, a great brand reputation is an essential recruiting and retention tool. This book shares practical strategies for protecting the brand and for preventing what the author calls involuntary brandslaughter.

Joe Tye, author of *The Florence Prescription: Accountability to Ownership* and (with Dr. Bob Dent) *Building a Culture of Ownership in Healthcare*

In this digital age that can move quickly, *The Illuminated Brand* is another straightforward, common sense and prescriptive book on how to protect and enhance your company's brand to keep up with the changing world.

Dave Kelley, Former COO/CIO TD Ameritrade, Former CTO Merrill Lynch, Corporate Executive Consultant

It takes time to build a brand to where it becomes valuable, and integrated, with your products and services. But it takes little time to become a liability. *The Illuminated Brand* gives you the strategies and game plan to ensure your brand remains an effective part of your success.

Harry Paul, Coauthor, *FISH! A Proven Way to Boost Morale and Improve Results*

This book is a must read. No surprise because David Corbin is one of the top business executives and innovators in America today. With his many years of practical experience, David has developed a wonderful ability to help companies, large and small, to quickly increase sales, profitability, and a culture of brand integrity. I have personally worked with David for more than 25 years, in a wide range of products and services. *The Illuminated Brand* is a roadmap to building your brand value.

> Brian Tracy, Professional Speaker,
> Author, Business Consultant

I created the Secret Knock with clear brand values, brand promises, and a specific vibe. I've learned early on from David Corbin, as he mentored me, that everything we do is either building our killing our brand. I read his previous book, *BrandSlaughter*. Now, in this business parable, *The Illuminated Brand,* he offers a SOLID program to implement immediately and to make sure that our brand is clear to all who represent it; how they want to live the brand each and every day and how to maintain that culture. Really, really good book.

> Dr. Greg Reid, founder Secret Knock,
> Author, Filmmaker

When I started the UGG business, it took me four years to figure out the correct steps in building the Brand and making it an international Icon. I wish I had *The Illuminated Brand* book back then, as it packed with solid tools to make sure that everyone in the organization "gets it" and "Lives the Brand."

> Brian Smith, UGG Founder

What this book does is BIG. It shows you how to build your brand asset value even under seemingly untenable conditions; the conditions of business as 'un'usual. The take-aways are profound, realistic, and actionable.

Rob Angel, Inventor of PICTIONARY!

Building a brand is tough. Getting the team to live the brand is tougher. And doing it under pressure? Crazy. This book shows you how.

Jeff Hoffman, Co-Founder, Priceline

We don't always equate an organization's brand with employee engagement. However, each and every employee is either enhancing their organization's brand or putting it at risk. David Corbin illuminates the critical components of identifying the organization's weaknesses, while also discovering and utilizing previously hidden strengths. When following this approach, your organization is best positioned for success.

Sharon Lechter, Author of *Think and Grow Rich for Women*, Co-author of *Exit Rich, Three Feet From Gold, Outwitting the Devil, Success and Something Greater, Rich Dad Poor Dad* and 14 other *Rich Dad* books

The Illuminated Brand offers Health Care Senior Leadership a glimpse at a roadmap to maintain brand integrity through adversity, both internal and external. A short parable about a hospital's journey through Covid and how maintaining brand integrity brought both cohesion and practical solutions to staff and senior leadership. Great read!

Annette Ridenour, President, Aesthetics, Inc.

It's time to learn the true meaning and definition of what it takes to develop a brand that excels during even the tests of time. It's time to up-level your value and learn the actual techniques to make your brand stand in such a positive way. Hats off to David M. Corbin for doing just that in his latest amazing book, *The Illuminated Brand.* He shares the step-by-step process in such a unique way that will be sure to bring you to that next critical level you have been desiring to achieve.

Erik "Mr. Awesome" Swanson
CEO & Founder of Habitude Warrior International, 10 Time #1
Best Selling Author ~Author of *The 13 Steps to Riches, Crush & Dominate, Social Millions*

After reading your book, *Illuminate,* I looked at my own skill set and found that I indeed have many skills that I can apply to my life, the lives of my teams, and my family. The actionable skills found in *The Illuminated Brand* have given me the outlook of a problem solver, which has significantly improved my value as a mentor to my teams, my tenants, and my family members, thereby enhancing every area of my personal life. I have recommended your books to every person that is important to me in my life.

Ray Speth, Businessman, Investor,
Health and Life Coach Extraordinaire

We've been through some tough times. Keeping afloat was the goal. But at the cost of the brand? How do you maintain the brand promise under these circumstances? Corbin's book teaches just that.

Michael Drew, NYTimes Best Seller Strategist,
Founder of Profluent

Branding is the most critical element in growing your business, and, in *The Illuminated Brand*, David has written the perfect guide to build and protect your brand. Learn to engage your employees and customers to further strengthen your brand, remain consistent in messaging, and more with *The Illuminated Brand!*

Marshall Goldsmith, New York Times #1 bestselling author of *Triggers, Mojo, and What Got You Here Won't Get You There.* Marshall Goldsmith - Thinkers 50 #1 Executive Coach and only two-time #1 Leadership Thinker in the world

In my fields of study, attention to detail and, at the same time, breaking it down to easy steps are critical. In this book, *The Illuminated Brand*, David Corbin did just that. The model that he exposes through application in the hospital shows that he "gets it," knows how cultures are formed and supported and the importance of performing and serving from shared values. His attention to detail is flawless. And the award goes to … David Corbin.

Richard Dreyfuss, Actor, Producer, Deeply Engaged Citizen and Patriotic Lover of The United States of America

Great writers know that the best way to teach important concepts is by telling a powerful story. *The Illuminated Brand* is the tale of a business struggling to protect its brand amidst the ruthless pressures of the pandemic. Corbin wraps this compelling story around his critical lesson of brand integrity. *The Illuminated Brand* is packed with information for business owners on how to stay true to their brand and to find, follow and fix problems, and it delivers those messages in an attention-grabbing fictional story.

Maria Crimi Speth, Attorney, Jaburg & Wilk, P.C.

As a 20-year veteran in M&A, I have been educating clients for decades on the positive & negative impact of "BRAND VALUE!" It's imperative to build and protect your company's brand, as it is one of the highest value drivers in maximizing the value of your business. The more well branded your company is, the more it will sell for! David Corbin's brilliant approach in his previous book, *BrandSlaughter*, and now in Corbin's sequel, *The Illuminated Brand*, he demystifies the mystery around growing and killing your company's brand. I strongly encourage you to read this extremely insightful and powerful book and start implementing these golden nuggets immediately. If done correctly, it's basically an insurance policy on increasing and protecting your brand value!

Michelle Seiler Tucker,

Founder & Ceo of Seiler Tucker Inc., M&AMI, CSBA, CM&AP, Best-Selling Author of *Sell Your Business For More Than It's Worth, Think and Grow Rich Today*, and *Exit Rich*, a *Wall Street Journal* and *USA Today* Best Seller! Host of Exit Rich Podcast

David's writings are informational and inspirational. His use of parables makes it easy to understand and implement. I always have at least one of David's books on my desk in the office and frequently re-read them when I need a "booster shot." Branding does not simply apply to our places of work. David has helped me to learn that the principles of branding also apply to each of us as individuals. Every one of us has the opportunity to utilize the information provided in his book to ensure that we are living up to the brand values that we wish to have. David has taught me that we have the ability to introspect and self-examine whether we are living up to these brand values every day. It is never about beating ourselves up when we fail. It is always about recognizing that we can be better than we were the day before. I am grateful that David continues to share his wisdom with us.

David Weisman, Ph.D., CPXP,
Chief Experience Officer NYC Health + Hospitals / Queens

The Illuminated Brand by David Corbin is the most powerful book (and concept) I've read about creating, growing, and maintaining a profitable successful business with long-term, invested employees. Corbin's concepts of Brand Courage, Brand Integrity and Involuntary Brandslaughter are pure gold to our bottom line. It reads like a fast-paced novel, while giving us the tools to Find It, Face It, Fix It. Every business leader and employee needs to read his books then ACT.

JR Green, Former CEO, Mountain States Mortgage

We're living in the most extraordinary period in human history. People have more options, greater access to information, and ever increasing expectations. Brand loyalty, which is anything but assured, must be earned and maintained. David Corbin tells us that the key to earning and maintaining brand loyalty is brand integrity. A brand is a promise. And to acquire and keep loyal customers, your customers must be able to depend on your brand to deliver on its promise. Integrity is what creates and maintains that commitment to the customer. A great and inspiring read. I highly recommend this book.

George J. Chanos, Chairman of Capriotti's;
Author of *Millennial Samurai: A Mindset for the 21st Century*. Former Attorney General of Nevada

Not your typical business book. I enjoyed how the fictional (but well-researched) story of a hospital brought home the importance of Brand Integrity and the Illumination process of Find It, Face It,

Fix It. It was clever how the book was able to weave Rejuvenation Station into the solution and how the book's heroes were unlikely ones. Setting up an ongoing process for employees to be heard and their input put into action is something many companies miss out on. *The Illuminated Brand* cleverly shows how any company can protect its reputation from BrandSlaughter, while improving employee satisfaction and reducing unwanted turnover.

Scott Birnbaum, CEO MORF AI,

Former VP Samsung Electronics

We live in an age where most brands have at least one highly comparable competitive brand. Oftentimes, the only difference in rational and emotional benefits is the experience a consumer has with the brand at any stage—digital or physical—pre-purchase consideration, purchase, usage, customer support, and any other "experience point." David's focus on developing awareness and engagement of all employees to truly understand the brand's ethos and experiential narrative at every "experience point" interaction is essential for brand survival in an age where the consumer is boss, and they have other brand choices.

Steven Cook, Former Samsung Electronics North America

CMO, P&G and Coca-Cola Global VP Strategic Marketing

How do you cut through all the clutter in the times we've been through? How do you stand out and not blend in so you're not perceived as just another slice in the loaf? Corbin's book, *The Illuminated Brand*, teaches just that and clearly demonstrates how to be a me-only brand in a me-too world!

Gerry Foster, President, Gerry Foster Branding

A short and inspiring story that exemplifies in so many ways the importance and power of our brand. The parable is timely and will also be timeless in its message on how each and every employee can make a difference in a company's brand. I was touched to tears several times as the story was very real. When things felt hopeless, the company did a brilliant job accessing the wisdom and power of its people to get through a very difficult time and honor the vision, mission, and brand of the organization.

Robin Blanc Mascari, Partner, Enlightened Networking LLC, Entrepreneur, Mentor, Trainer, Leader, Coach, Talk Show Host

chapter one

The auditorium was packed for the annual Audit of Brand Integrity award ceremony. Vivian walked across the stage and gently put the Briggs Award for Brand Integrity, commonly called BABI, on the podium until it was presented to this year's recipient by Phillip, Reliance Hospital's CEO.

As head of the Human Resources Department, Vivian had been in charge of brand integrity training for the hospital since they'd adopted the audit 14 years before. It had become so ingrained in their mission and core values that it was as important as the hospital's accreditation. And for good reason—when the hospital was in integrity with its brand, they were confident they were in compliance with the highest standards in health care.

After glancing at the clock, Vivian nodded at Phillip, signifying that she was ready to open the ceremony. Gathering her notes, she walked to the podium and welcomed their guests, who were all Reliance employees. Among them were surgeons, department directors, doctors and nurses, support staff, security guards, and maintenance personnel. To Reliance, every department and every employee played a vital role in keeping their brand alive.

Today, five employees would receive OBI awards. These were awards for exemplifying Outstanding Brand Integrity. All were carefully selected from a cross section of the departments within the hospital. Only one, however, would receive the prestigious BABI, the Briggs Award for Brand Integrity, named after Walker Briggs, who was, in many ways, a legend at the hospital. Walker had been chief of Security until he had retired seven years before, and he was known and loved by everyone who knew him. Standing only five and a half feet tall, he wasn't a large man by any means, but he had a huge presence. It was Walker Briggs who represented the hospital's brand in everything he had done. It was his smiling face that greeted employees, patients, visitors, and vendors as they walked through the doors every morning. Walker lived the brand. He was the brand. And that is precisely why the highest award had been named after him.

"As we mark the 14th year of celebrating brand integrity, it's important to remember the purpose of the brand audit and why we do it. We all know that when we are out of integrity with our brand, which is to provide clinical excellence, superior quality, safety, and compassion to our patients and the community we serve, we can be assured that we are meeting the highest standards of healthcare and providing for the needs of our community," Vivian announced.

"This year's awards recipients were nominated by their supervisors and peers and voted upon by our Board of Directors," she continued before introducing each board member.

"The full report of our 2020 audit is now available on our website, which is a testament to our commitment to be as transparent as possible. I am proud to say that the results show that we have continued to meet our high expectations, and Reliance Hospital is in brand integrity!" to which the audience applauded. The annual audit was a big deal—a very big deal—and every department worked very hard to ensure that they were aligned with the hospital's brand and values.

"Presenting this year's awards is Phillip, our Chief Executive Officer. Phillip …"

"Good morning, everyone, and thank you, Vivian. You have been the face of brand integrity here at Reliance since its inception. I would like to publicly commend you for ensuring that every employee receives the proper training to help us meet our goals, as well as the hard work you've put in to prepare for today's ceremony," Phillip said. "As most of you know, we started auditing brand integrity shortly after I came to Reliance, and Vivian has been instrumental in its implementation---so much so that she has been award the Briggs Award for Brand Integrity, as well."

"Today, I congratulate each and every one of you for your dedication and commitment to our brand and the exemplary way you have lived and breathed our brand while performing your duties. This ceremony is one way of thanking you, but in order to thank all employees, we will be providing free meals to employees on all shifts for the next seven days."

Now, turning our attention to our awards, I want you to know that there were many who deserve to be honored today, but only five can receive the OBI award. The selection process was particularly tough this year, which is fantastic. The individuals chosen to receive awards for outstanding brand integrity are

Anne Tazzmore, Don Garwood, Libby Eitan and Chester Balzak. I would like to personally congratulate each of you for surpassing expectations and being stellar representatives of our brand. Again, congratulations," Phil said as the crowd applauded.

"Every year, one individual is chosen to receive the BABI, the Briggs Award for Brand Integrity. Named after Walker Briggs, it is an award bestowed upon the employee who represents our brand at all times. The recipient is chosen not only for their performance, but also for their effort, cooperation, compassion, and care. While it was difficult to select just five individuals to receive awards for outstanding brand integrity, I must say it was not difficult to determine the winner of this year's BABI. Ladies and gentlemen, I hereby award the Walker Briggs Award for Brand Integrity to none other than Dr. Alexander Barrett, our chief cardiac surgeon and one of Walker's biggest fans.

In accepting his award, Dr. Barrett acknowledged everyone in his department, as well as all employees, for he said it was they who made it possible for him to win this award. Most of all, though, he thanked Walker Briggs.

"Walker was the first face I saw when I walked through these doors 12 years ago," he said. "He didn't just live the brand—he *was* the brand. It took me some time to catch onto the principle of brand integrity and buy into it. Walker was the one who opened my eyes and showed me what brand integrity really meant and why it was important. Because of him, I stand before you today. As a personal and close friend of Walker's, I know how much each of you meant to him and how much he valued the years spent here at Reliance. It was a labor of love for him, I assure you. And that's what brand integrity is … a labor of love for our professions and the people we care for."

As the audience applauded, Dr. Barrett cleared his throat before proceeding.

"I graciously accept this award and am honored to have earned your trust and respect. I am also humbled to now be among the employees who have previously been BABI recipients. Walker Briggs was the first recipient and deservedly so. Some who knew me years ago might argue that I should be the last person to receive this award. Back then, they were right. I admit I was, shall we say, standoffish? In my mind, I didn't have the time to care about anything but my patients. But Walker never let that stand in the way, and without fail, he was nothing but professional, kind, helpful, and dependable to me. It wasn't until Walker Briggs became my patient that I became aware of the importance of brand integrity and how it affects not only me and my patients, but this entire hospital. Only then was I able to reciprocate that treatment and level of support, and I owe it all to Walker. To be given an award that is named after the man who personified brand integrity is, indeed, a great and humbling honor. To receive this award today is even more special, though, because the man for whom it was named is no longer with us. As I shared with Phillip and Vivian early this morning, our friend and coworker, Walker Briggs, passed away in his sleep last night. Looking out at your wonderful faces, I know that he will live on here at Reliance Hospital. He made a lasting mark on every one of us and was loved by so many in the community. Not only is it an honor to receive this award, but it was an even greater honor to know and love the man for whom it was named," the doctor said, as he raised his BABI up above his head. "Thank you, Walker … Thank you, everyone."

chapter two

 Monday morning signified the weekly meeting of the administrators of Reliance Hospital. Phillip looked around the table, making sure everyone was present before providing a recap of the weekend.

"A gunshot victim was brought into the Emergency Department Friday night, and per our policy and in accord with the police department, we went into immediate lockdown, which passed without incident," he announced. "Reports indicate we had longer than average wait times in the ED on Saturday afternoon. Richard, will you look into that and get back to me when you know why and if it could have been prevented? I do see that multiple victims of an automobile accident were brought in earlier; perhaps we were still recovering from that influx."

Phillip then received updates on several projects, including the construction of their latest urgent care center, which would be located in a town about 15 miles north of the hospital. It would be the fifth urgent care facility the hospital would open under their mission to make health care more accessible, while devoting the emergency department to actual emergencies, at least as much as possible. He then reported on the status of their senior memory care center, which was being constructed a half mile down the street. Reliance had done a great deal of expansion under Phillip's watch, but it was just a start in their ten-year plan.

"Okay, anyone have any questions or any other business to report?" he asked.

A few "no's" were mumbled as chairs were pushed away from the conference table. As people shuffled their papers and picked up their coffee cups, preparing to leave, Richard Blackburn, the hospital's chief medical officer, spoke.

"Hey, has anyone heard anything about the U.S. potentially getting hit with a new virus?" he asked.

"What are you talking about?" Phillip asked.

"Well, I hear that the government has been notified that there's a novel virus overseas, and there are concerns that it could reach pandemic level. Even worse, a treatment hasn't been found for it. If this is true and the virus enters the States, it could be unlike anything we've ever seen before."

"Rich, is your source reliable?" Phillip asked.

"Well, he is a relative, but he also works for an agency with three letters, if you know what I mean," Richard replied.

"Top secret stuff, huh? Well, I guess we'll have to wait and see how this plays out," commented Tracy, their chief financial officer.

"Wait, wait a minute," interjected Duncan Edwards, Reliance's chief auditor of brand integrity. "What if this actually happens? Are we prepared to handle it? I think we might want to be proactive here, rather than reactive. If this virus is real and it's as bad as you say it could be, there's got to be something we can do to prepare for it."

"Like what?" Vivian, VP of HR asked.

"That's what we need to find out. Are we prepared for a potential pandemic? Do we have enough beds? Enough equipment and supplies? Where are we weakest?" Duncan answered.

"If we don't know anything about the virus, how can we prepare for it?" Tracy asked. "Sure, there are some things we can do, but we might just have to wait and hope for the best. After all, it might not even come to fruition at all."

"You know, I just read a book that deals with that very thing. It's called *Illuminate*, and it's about the positive power of negative thinking," Duncan said.

"What? The positive of power of negative thinking? What does that even mean?" Phillip asked.

"Well, in a nutshell, we all know about the trend to focus on the positive, not the negative, right? But here's the thing. The book states that if we ignore the negative stuff, it won't go away. It will, however, build up and grow, like a cancer, and it could ultimately be our downfall. You can't just sweep things under the rug and hope nobody else sees it. Ignoring or hiding something won't make it go away. We can't just wait it out and hope for the best."

"So what does the book propose we do?" asked Richard.

"It's a three-step process. The author calls it 'Face it, Follow it, Fix it.' First, you find and **face** the negative issues, whether they are in policies, personnel, supplies, whatever. Next you **follow** it. Essentially you shine a light on potential issues, instead of sweeping them under the proverbial rug and hoping they don't cause any problems. You follow it back into the past as to where it came from, what caused it and what's keeping it alive. You also follow it into the future to see what happens if you **don't** deal with it. Then you do what you have to do to **fix** it or at least reduce its negative impact," advised Duncan.

"Really? This sounds interesting, Duncan. I can see that there is a correlation here with brand integrity where we face, follow and fix areas where we are out of synch. I also think you make a good point—if we wait and see what happens and we **do** get hit with a pandemic, it could be BrandSlaughter if we're not ready for it," Phillip remarked.

"I think you're right. You know, I wouldn't have brought this up if my source hadn't sounded so serious. It takes a lot to scare him, but not to panic anyone, I detected some fear in his voice," Duncan admitted.

"No, Duncan, you're right. We need to be prepared for this, or any potential pandemic or health crisis, for that matter. If it doesn't happen, great, at least we will know we've *illuminated* it to lessen the impact if it ever does and we'll be prepared if something does happen in the future. We owe it to our patients, our staff, and the community," said Phillip. "Richard and Duncan, can you clear your calendars and be in my office at 8:00 tomorrow morning, so we can come up with a plan? Vivian, you should probably be there, too. This is something we should have done long ago. If there's even a remote possibility that this threat is real, we can't afford to waste any time."

"I'll be there. I'm sure I speak for everyone when I say that I hope we don't have a pandemic. But if we can make sure that we're in brand integrity when it comes to things we *can* control, there has to got to be a way to make sure we can stay in integrity when it comes to things we *cannot* control," Duncan said.

"The last thing we want to do is to commit *involuntary* brandslaughter," added Dr. Barrett, their chief cardiovascular surgeon. "I've been guilty of brandslaughter in the past; luckily, Walker helped me shine a light on it and I was able to face it, follow it and fix it."

"Involuntary brandslaughter … " Vivian mused. "I like that. We know how to respond when things happen in the normal course of business, but a pandemic—that's something that happens at us, something we certainly didn't sign up for. And that's as involuntary as it gets. Phillip, it looks like we've got work to do."

"Yes, we do, and we need to start today. Rich, see if you can learn anything else about this virus, confidentially, of course. Use whatever connections you might have. And Duncan, send me the link to that book, *Illuminate*. I'll order a few copies for us today, if I can. We need to make sure we're all on the same page."

chapter three

 All department heads convened, filling the boardroom at Reliance Hospital. Word had gotten around, as it often does, and the news of a potential pandemic summoned up speculation and conjecture about what was coming down the pike. Different theories were passed back and forth, followed by predictions of mass casualties and grave illness on an unprecedented scale.

The buzz silenced when Phillip and Vivian entered the room.

"Please, everyone, be seated. We've got a lot of ground to cover, so let's get started right away," their CEO said.

"As you all know, we've worked hard to build our metrics to fulfill our mission with authenticity, reliability, and vulnerability. As you might also know, we are here today for a very specific reason. There are substantiated claims that there is a novel virus overseas. While we don't know much about this virus, there is the potential that it will impact us. We don't know how, and we don't know when. We do know that there is no vaccine, and, at this time, we aren't aware of a treatment protocol," Phillip shared.

"So if we don't know anything about it, what can we do?"

"That's a good question, and that is precisely why I called you all here today. I'm aware that there we don't have the answers, and I don't expect us to—not yet, anyway. I think we can all acknowledge that we don't have the resources of time, money, or even the knowledge to deal with a potential pandemic, which is what we are facing, but being in integrity with our brand, we know that we are brave enough to capture and address potential tough issues now, before they become crises, instead of sweeping them under the rug and hoping we don't ever had to address them," replied Phillip.

"We are being confronted with something unique. We have never had a similar threat of this magnitude for which no one is prepared. In fact, while, of course, I hope it doesn't happen, we might find that we've never experienced anything like it in our lifetime. This could have a major impact on us, and because of that and our responsibility to the community and our staff, it is important that we protect ourselves from what Dr. Barrett has called *"involuntary* brandslaughter," Phillip continued. "This means that we need to be proactive. We need to illuminate; to face, follow and fix whatever and wherever we can. We'll have to identify our weaknesses across all departments and address them. Do I have any volunteers to head this effort?"

Duncan Edwards, the chief auditor of brand integrity, was the first to volunteer.

"Thank you, Duncan, but I can't pull you from ABI. If we do experience a pandemic, your role with the audits of brand integrity will be more critical than ever. You will play an integral part in both efforts, I assure you. Now, do I have another volunteer?"

"I'll do it," offered Vivian, the senior VP of Human Resources. "I've been involved with ABI training since its inception, and I think I am well versed in it."

"Perfect, Vivian. To get started, I'd like to hear your thoughts," said Phillip.

"I think we need to lean on The Illuminated Brand program, and anticipate areas that this, I guess I'll refer to it as a pandemic, will impact, go back and revisit our values and our intended brand descriptors and see how they will be impacted. From there, we need to break up into groups. Does anyone else remember when we did this?" Vivian asked.

"I wasn't there," said Greg Hicks, the head of the emergency department. "However, I've heard a lot about that program from other staff members."

"Okay, here's a recap and you'll get why it's called The Illuminated Brand Program. To start off, we made a list of our values and our intended brand descriptors—how we want people to describe our brand. Then we broke our team into cross-functional groups. In that endeavor, we first discussed the intersections of contact we have with our patients, our patient's families, caregivers, vendors, and all those we are in contact with on a frequent basis. So we have the list of values, intended descriptors and the touchpoints with all the other people. And, with that list, we next discussed the areas where we were performing in integrity with our values and where we were indeed earning our brand descriptors. Basically, taking inventory of those areas where we are really *living* the brand."

Across the table, someone spoke up.

"I remember—that was actually fun. It felt good seeing the positive impact we were having."

"Well, do you remember what happened when we got to the *next* part, when we got serious about where we were **out** of sync with our values and brand descriptors?" Vivian asked.

"Oh, don't remind me. That part was certainly *not* fun."

"I know it wasn't. But here's the thing—we did it. We authentically and courageously illuminated. We pushed through it and got it done, and we learned a lot," Vivian replied.

"What happened?" asked Greg.

"It was quite interesting. At that point, each of the groups reported back and gave examples of where we were **undermining** our values and were out of sync with our brand descriptors. I always thought of that as being brand courageous," she laughed.

"Hell, yes, it was," Phillip interjected. "We had to illuminate the negatives, all of them, and that self-assessment was an eye opener."

"Oh, I remember," Vivian agreed. "But even though it was a solemn report, I believe everyone felt a sigh of relief that something they observed and didn't know how to fix was actually being confronted. And of course, as you recall, the next round of discussions took place over time and in all department areas where we worked on troubleshooting and created SBI's."

"You lost me again," said Rich.

"Those are our Strategic Brand Initiatives, Rich. SBI's. As a group, as a team, we all focused on finding solutions to the specific issues. Closing the gaps between where we were and where we wanted to be. That's where the magic happened."

"Right," Duncan added. "That's the beauty of the Illuminated Brand Program. Nobody likes to hear about problems. Remember what we've always been told … focus on the positive, not the negative. Well, that was a bit of a disservice. Truth is, the negative stuff doesn't just vanish because we wish it to … if anything, when it's ignored, it has the potential to grow and create havoc, something none of us want, especially if we do have a pandemic."

"Remember what Walker Briggs used to say?" Phillip asked rhetorically. "Negative issues are like mushrooms. Keep 'em in the dark and they thrive and multiply!"

"Like you've always said, Duncan, we can't solve everything we face, but we can't solve anything unless we face it," Vivian smiled, adding to the banter across the room.

"Well, just how did you face it?"

"First, we broke into those groups—some cross departmental and others departmental, illuminated each of the issues, and created those SBI's, the strategic brand initiatives. To do that, we asked ourselves, 'How can we reduce the problem or eliminate it altogether so we can fully engage in brand and values integrity in all of these problem areas?'"

"The goal is for *all* the issues, but realistically, at this point in time, we want to aim for *most* issues," Phillip said. "It's a constant work in process."

"So how are we going to approach this novel virus that we may or may not deal with?" asked the new ED head. "We don't even know if it's going to come here—or not. I mean, we could be wasting a lot of time and effort for something that doesn't even happen. Sorry, but this is really tough for me to sign on to. I mean, c'mon."

"If it is coming or it isn't, that doesn't really matter. But don't you think we will all feel better knowing we covered the bases, anticipated areas which might be massively impacted and, therefore, are as prepared as we can possibly be? The good thing is, even if it doesn't occur, we will have done the discovery and the work should we encounter a situation like this in the future, whether it's a pandemic or any other type of major challenge," Phillip explained.

"Okay, I get *that*. But we have so many unknowns and other things to deal with. Why would we chase ghosts that we can't see and that might never make themselves known?" Greg asked. "I'm not trying to be difficult here. But I do want to point out that what you're asking everyone to do could be exhaustive, especially if we experience a large influx of seriously ill patients. I may be wrong, but I think you're asking too much of our staff. I'm just sayin'."

"Well, let me answer your question with a question," Phillip replied. "What if we ignore those ghosts that are lurking in our departments and our practices, and they actually **do** come back to haunt us? How might that impact our staff? They would be devastated for being caught blind-sided. And that's exactly why it's imperative that we deal with this now. Hopefully, you can get on board and agree that we need to illuminate our weaknesses now, before it's too late, because if we don't, we might just find that they have a catastrophic effect later—on our patients, our community, our hospital and, yes, on our staff. I'd rather err on the side of caution than to live with the fact that people suffered because we downplayed this threat. Believe me, when it comes to the loss of lives, nobody wants to be guilty of brandslaughter, voluntary or involuntary."

The weight of Phillip's words was met with silence by his group of administrators.

"Okay, so are there any other questions or comments?" he asked.

When no one responded, he turned to Vivian.

"Okay, Vivian. I have to leave for a zoom meeting with the board of directors. I'm confident you can take it from here," he said before walking out of the room, as Vivian got to work and started dividing the team into groups.

"Who do we have here from Housekeeping? Clinical? Dietary? Scheduling? Let's form our committees and select a facilitator for each one before we adjourn," she said.

chapter four

Nearly a month later, news of a potential pandemic was no longer a hushed rumor, but it had been the topic of mainstream news coverage on a daily basis. Reporters quoted statistics of confirmed cases in countries across the world, and to anyone listening, it was apparent that it was only a matter of time before it would reach the States. Like hospitals across the nation, Reliance had been busy preparing for the expected pandemic and the unknowns that would come with it.

Vivian's committees had identified crucial areas that needed to be addressed, regardless of when or how the pandemic played out. First, personal protective equipment would be needed in abundant quantities for staff, patients, and visitors. Mass quantities had been ordered, but it appeared that there was already a shortage of medical masks because the public, as well as healthcare institutions, were stocking up … just in case.

A great deal wasn't known about the virus, but initial findings showed that it attacked the respiratory system. For that reason, they would need a large supply of pulse oximeters at minimum — and in the worst-case scenario, they could potentially need respirators, oxygen concentrators and/or ventilators for a large percentage of their hospital beds. It was preparing for the worst-case scenario that was daunting. Not only did it tap heavily into their budget, but their illumination process showed that PPE and medical supplies were just the tip of the iceberg. If the virus was as contagious as it was believed to be, it would affect not only the community, but their doctors, nurses, technicians, therapists, housekeepers—virtually every hospital employee would be susceptible, which could have a devastating impact on their ability to serve their community at a time when it was needed most.

Vivian led the charge in making sure the hospital would be adequately staffed. As-needed clinicians became part-time employees, and interviews were underway to hire more as-needed workers to step up if shortages occurred. Resources were shifted to accommodate the addition of more than a dozen additional housekeepers for every shift to make sure super sanitation issues were addressed.

As part of those sanitation measures, there would now only be one designated entrance to the hospital, and Security was charged with the responsibility of screening everyone who came through those doors. Patients, visitors, and employees alike had to be masked upon entrance. Hand sanitizing was required prior to entering, and only those with a normal temperature were allowed in public spaces.

These changes brought with them anxiety. A fear of the unknown was a very real thing, and it touched upon nearly all of Reliance's employees, especially administrators and department heads who were charged with protecting the health and safety of the employees and the community. There was only one managerial leader who openly voiced disagreement over what he deemed "overkill." Greg Hicks, the director of the emergency department, still wasn't totally on board. Yes, he had been following news of the pandemic, but to him it was all an exercise … maybe one of futility. His greatest concern was that preparing for what might not happen would put unnecessary strain on the resources of the emergency department. Making this the first point of contact for the public also placed undue stress on his already overworked staff.

When voicing those concerns, he told Vivian, "I have no reason to believe that we won't be able to deal with whatever we are confronted with. We are doctors and nurses. That's what we do. We deal with whatever we are faced with when it walks through the door—but we don't strain our existing resources because something just might come through the door."

That was precisely what he told his brother-in-law, Kevin. Kevin was a paramedic, and as a first responder, he understood emergency medicine. Over the years, the two men had had many discussions about the changes and expectations in providing emergency care and for the most part, they were in agreement on the issues. They had no control over how many patients they would serve in a day. They were faced with triaging, diagnosing and treating patients at a rapid pace—often in life-and-death situations. On top of that, they dealt with anxious and upset family members and from time to time, had to deal with individuals who could place themselves or their coworkers in life-threatening situations.

But it was precisely that—the unknowns, the ever-changing routine, people, and situations—that got their adrenaline flowing. It was a rush and, in part, was what made them love their jobs and kept them dedicated to coming back to it every day, regardless of what that day might entail.

So maybe it was natural that something like a pandemic didn't scare Dr. Hicks. The unknown and risks were part of his daily life, maybe even in his DNA. It was why he'd chosen his specialty, and why he was so darn good at it.

Greg's leadership and abilities were highly respected across the hospital. He did his job, and he did it well. No one could or would argue that. However, Greg's reluctance to face this potential crisis was a concern, not only for Vivian and Phil, but also for some of the technicians and nurses who worked side by side with him in the ED. Greg wasn't scared of a virus—he'd dealt with them throughout his entire career. But not everyone felt the same. They were quite frightened for what the future might hold, but their fear was silenced by their reluctance to meet with their supervisor's disproval and disappointment. Greg was the departmental rapport leader, dominated the culture and, well, they just didn't want to rattle his cage.

The highly esteemed emergency department director wouldn't face the fact that there could be potential issues down the road. He had absolutely no idea that his staff felt vulnerable and frightened. Even worse, he had no idea that he was at risk of committing involuntary brandslaughter in the highest degree. Until these things were brought to light, Dr. Hicks would remain in the dark.

chapter five

Vivian and Duncan were holding their weekly ABI meeting. The agenda on this day was to review the areas that were identified by the hospital's departments as potential brandslaughter hotspots during the most recent audit. Most of the revelations weren't surprising. An expected increase in the demand for personal protective equipment was predictable, and a shortage could be prevented … unless their suppliers couldn't meet the demand. Vivian placed a check next to this item, indicating an area where Reliance might involuntarily jeopardize their brand integrity. A shortage of staff in all areas could potentially occur, and they even believed that their mechanical heating and cooling systems could spread the virus through recirculated air. Upgrading those systems would be costly and cause a budget shortfall. After all, such expenditures were usually reserved for proposal in a multi-year strategic plan that would occur in phases. This was one area that the two department heads were in agreement on. If there was one area where they were most likely to be lacking during a pandemic, it was the one where there weren't sufficient funds or time to be proactive.

But Duncan and Vivian didn't anticipate another thing that was out of their control—an area where the hospital would eventually become reactive, rather than proactive—and that was public anxiety. That anxiety entered their doors before there were any signs of a pandemic.

"What is going on?" Dr. Hicks asked out loud one afternoon. It had been unusually busy that day with a notably high number of patients coming into the emergency department. It happened a few times a year, but usually only during the peak of the flu season, with the exception of the occasional major accident or rare disaster, such as an explosion or the train derailment that injured 17 people four years before. But this was different. There hadn't been any major incidents causing an upswell in incoming patients—and most of the patients weren't even critically ill. If there was any common thread among them, it was that the majority of the patients were mildly ill (if at all) … some had a low-grade fever, while others suffered from a cough or nagging headache. They weren't there because they were in dire need of medical attention—no, they were there because they were *afraid* that they were going to be in dire need of treatment.

"Dr. Hicks," one of the emergency room technicians approached him, "I just opened the last case of masks. At this rate, I'm afraid we won't have enough to get through the weekend."

"Did you check the supply room?" he asked.

"Yes, sir. I know there were three cases there at the beginning of the week, but they're all gone," she said.

"Thanks for letting me know. I'll take care of it," he said with a sigh. He was simply too busy to have to deal with such issues, but it was one more thing thrust on his all too full plate that day.

By the time his shift was over, he was more than ready to go home and put his feet up, but he couldn't. He simply couldn't walk away without bringing matters to the attention of the higher ups. In his opinion, they needed to know that they created a monster and they were going to have to deal with it. It was time to have a talk.

"Sit down, Greg," Phillip said, motioning toward an empty chair. They were in the CEO's conference room and Phil had invited Vivian, Duncan, and the chief medical officer to join them for the impromptu meeting. "Tell us what's on your mind."

"That's exactly what I came here to do," Dr. Hicks said. "For starters, has anyone noticed the number of patients coming through the ED today? It seems everybody in the county is bringing in their mother, their three-year-old, and their grandma. They're all acting like they're going to die and *demanding* to be given priority treatment. I mean, to hell with the guy in the next room who is having chest pains! And do you know why? Because there *might* be a pandemic! Everybody and their brother is panicking, and, I gotta tell ya, I think the fault lies with you!"

"Wait a minute, Greg—our fault? How do you figure?" Vivian asked, making sure she used a calm, non-defensive tone.

"Yes. I knew this was going to happen. And I hate to say I told you so, but I told you so. You all heard the word 'pandemic' and you got trigger happy and scurried around like the sky was going to fall. It's that type of reaction that has the media in a frenzy, which is why people are coming through our doors in droves because they're afraid they've got this disease and they're going to die."

"Oh, but I'm not done. My staff has had one helluva day, and I have to tell you that your new rules have Security running circles. They have enough to do without having to take temperatures and telling people who can and who cannot come in. It's chaos down there, and I'm sorry but you're all guilty of creating it. You overreacted, and now everyone else is overreacting, too. On top of that, one of my techs informed me that we're on our last case of masks. What the hell? How is my department supposed to treat people who are sick and have open wounds if we don't have enough masks?"

"Greg, I can see you're upset," Phil replied. "And perhaps rightly so. But I think if we work together, these are issues we can all address. Let's start with the most urgent need—masks."

It was Duncan who chimed in.

"When we started the involuntary brandslaughter audit, identifying potential areas where a pandemic might shift us out of brand integrity, PPE was a serious concern across nearly every department. We immediately placed a large order, stocking our inventory for the near future. Since then, we've learned that our purchase order is on backorder due to high demand. Until then, masks are being distributed on an as-needed basis based on past use. We will, of course, continually reassess those needs and adjust accordingly. Now, let me see. Greg, it looks like we just gave you three cases—1,500 masks—just a few days ago. Your numbers can't be that high. Where did they go?"

"I don't have any idea where they are. I just know that at the rate we're going now, and since we have to give every patient and accompanying family member a mask on top of what our staff needs, we won't have enough to get through the weekend. The worst part is, it isn't even necessary. There is no pandemic—at least not yet, but here we are, overreacting and treating everyone like they have the plague. I saw this coming, and I warned you that it wasn't necessary. So, what are you going to do about it?" Dr. Hicks looked around the table, waiting for an answer.

"Duncan, will you make sure the ED has a sufficient number of masks to get through the weekend?" Phillip asked. "And Vivian, can you ask the business office to contact our supplier to see when we can expect our order? If they can't fill the order, go outside of our contract and find another supplier."

"Thank you," Greg sighed.

"And Dr. Hicks, I just want to remind you that this isn't anybody's 'fault.' It's the result of something that is beyond our control. You're not alone---we're all going to encounter unique situations and experience some trying times if this pandemic hits. And I have to disagree with you: the time to act is now, *before* we have staff shortages, critically ill patients, and a crisis on our hands," Phil pointed out.

His words were met with momentary silence, before Dr. Hicks stood up and said, "Thank you for listening, and keep me updated on the PPE status."

"I intend to do just that," Phil said as he reached for the phone and dialed the hospital's chief of security.

The next morning, the chief of security sent Phil a video. The night before, his staff had scanned hours of video, focusing on the emergency department. Their mission: to identify any video that could disclose what was happening with the department's PPE supply. Watching the video, Phil knew they had a problem. Visitors to the department were helping themselves to masks, often by the handful, as they shoved them into their purses and pockets. Phil also noted a few nurses who were putting on fresh PPE with exceeding frequency. But it was the last clip that caught him by surprise, as he watched a well-respected physician on the hospital staff throw boxes of surgical masks in his bag on two different occasions, before walking through the automatic doors and entering the elevator.

chapter six

 Word of their first confirmed case spread quickly. Phillip was notified just before 5 a.m. that an 81-year-old male who had been admitted the day before due to breathing difficulties had tested positive for the virus. Thanking the administrator on duty, Phillip advised her that it was business as usual. They had prepared for this, and there was no reason for panic.

It was the staff, however, that ran with the news. Text messages alerted employees hospital wide, both at work and at home, that they had their first case. The pandemic had struck Reliance Hospital and the community, and the reality produced a fear that could be seen and felt.

PPE covered medical and custodial staff from head to toe, leaving their eyes the only thing visible to patients and coworkers alike. Nurses treated patients from an arm's length if possible—that is, if the nurse hadn't called off that day. As predicted, staff shortages were quickly becoming an issue. While some employees chose to work long hours to deliver the care needed to their patients, others had chosen another option—calling off work. Calls offs among direct care staff rose by 20 percent virtually overnight.

The emergency department wasn't exempt, especially since its staff knew that any additional cases would definitely come through their doors. It was inevitable that Dr. Hicks's staff would be exposed to the virus. They had known that all along, but now that the first case had been confirmed, it wasn't a possibility any longer. It was a reality … one that was difficult for some employees to accept.

Dr. Hicks sighed and shook his head as he entered the doors, wondering how it was that the emergency department was swamped, while the rest of the hospital looked like a ghost town. The difference was stark, and the ramifications fell squarely on his shoulders.

The one thing he and Phillip did agree on was that it was business as usual. Illness and injuries didn't take time off; there were people in need of treatment every hour of the day and every day of the week. Pandemic or not, they had a job to do.

He quickly learned that everyone wasn't on board with that stance.

The phones hadn't stopped ringing all morning with calls from the public asking what they needed to do to get tested for the virus. Backlash ensued when they learned that only people with active symptoms were being tested. Their pleas to be an exception to the rule were heard. *My parents are elderly; I need to know it's okay to be around them. You don't understand—I work with little children!* and *I am diabetic, asthmatic, or have heart problems* were all futile attempts to get bumped to the front of the line for testing. While staff did everything they could to sympathize with their angst, their compassion did little to put their mind at ease.

On the other hand, patients who entered the emergency department with no symptoms *had* to be tested, even if they were there for totally unrelated reasons. To Greg Hicks, none of it made sense, medically or logically.

The only thing that did make sense was to keep his department running as smoothly as possible. He made it clear to his staff that it was business as usual.

Until it wasn't.

Shift change came in the middle of his day, relieving the tired personnel who had been there for 12 long hours. Usually shift change was unremarkable and went by without notice. This day was different, however, and it had a direct impact on the emergency department and its patients.

Emergency responders had just brought in two victims of an automobile accident, and Dr. Hicks was busy assessing their injuries when he learned that they had a patient who was experiencing breathing difficulty and complaining of a cough and sore throat. He had just called radiology to X-ray what he suspected to be a broken leg and was ruling out possible internal injuries of one of the accident victims when he was informed.

"Put her in room seven," he instructed. "And have Andrea do the initial assessment."

"I would, Doctor, but Andrea isn't here."

"She's not? Where is she?"

"She called off, sir. The staffing coordinator is going down the on-call list to get another RN here as soon as possible," the technician advised.

"Great," he said, not turning his head from his patient. "How about Kristy? Is she here?"

"Yes, she is."

"Okay, have her do it, and I'll be there when I'm finished here."

Twenty minutes later, he walked into room 7, expected to see Kristy tending to the patient. But instead, he was greeted by Rusty, a male nurse. After looking over the notes and the patient's vitals, Dr. Hicks examined the woman and ordered a chest x-ray.

"It's routine," he assured the patient. "I think you have a mild case of bronchitis. If that's the case, I'll prescribe you an antibiotic and something to relieve your cough."

After walking out of the room, he stopped Rusty, asking where Kristy was.

"Ummm, I think she's in the break room," Rusty answered, almost reluctantly.

A quick trip to the break room confirmed Rusty's words. Dr. Hicks peered his head into the door to see Kristy, in full PPE, being comforted by one of the techs as she wiped her tears.

"What's going on here?" he asked. "What's wrong?"

The tech was silent and looked to Kristy to reply.

"I, I just can't do it," she finally sobbed. "I just can't. I tried. I really did. But I'm too scared."

"Kristy, it's your *job*. You don't have a choice," Dr. Hicks replied.

A moment of uncomfortable silence passed before Kristy responded.

"Then I quit. I'm sorry, Dr. Hicks, but I'm pregnant. I just can't expose myself to the virus. My baby is more important than my job!" she wailed, before standing and walking out of the door.

The unexpected turn of events shocked Dr. Hicks and the tech, but it was Dr. Hicks who broke the silence.

"Let's get back to work," was all he said as he turned on his heels and walked back into the emergency department, as if nothing had happened.

For the rest of the day, Dr. Hicks noticed that the staff was subdued and unusually quiet. Usually a cheerful team, he caught them a few times in tight circles, whispering among themselves. He knew he could approach them and address their questions and concerns, but he had better things to do.

He had a pandemic to handle, one that had spiraled out of hand. Because it was causing his department a staff shortage and instilling fear into some of their best team members, it was putting the public at risk. In his mind, it was also putting Reliance Hospital at risk, as well. In his mind, though, he had done everything he could … to no avail. He'd tried, but in his opinion, he could talk until the pandemic was over, and nobody would listen.

Another week passed before Dr. Hicks knew he couldn't be silent a moment longer. Instead of getting better, his staffing difficulties had gotten significantly worse. And he blamed it on yet another new pandemic guideline: if a staff member had any symptoms whatsoever, they couldn't come to work until they had a negative test result or quarantined at home for two weeks.

Trying times tested him more often than he cared to admit, but it was an unexpected observation that made him realize it was time to address the situation. The department was particularly busy that afternoon when an ambulance brought in an individual with abdominal pains. Hearing his name, Dr. Hicks turned to see his brother-in-law, Kevin.

"Hey, Greg, you too busy to say hi?" he teased.

"To be honest, yes. It's a madhouse just about every day lately," he admitted.

"You aren't kidding," Kevin said, looking around at the people standing in strategic spots, waiting their turn while keeping their distance. "What's the wait time, anyway?"

"Longer than it should be, Kev."

"What happened? I mean, I know there's a pandemic and everything but ... Greg, you've always been able to keep things under control, even when it's chaotic. But this," he said, opening his arms wide to span the area, "this doesn't seem like you. Isn't there anything you can do about it?"

"I don't know, but I think it's time to try."

Sitting across Vivian's desk, Greg Hicks shared his staffing woes.

"I've dealt with it the best I can, but people are complaining, and it's affecting Reliance's reputation. We've got to do something about it ... and soon. The panic and policies are hurting us. I feared that would happen, and I believe I even predicted it," he said.

"Greg, we have no choice but to follow guidelines, and believe me, we are all just as frustrated with them. But we are liable and responsible for containing this virus as much as humanly possible," Vivian explained. "Yes, we have staff shortages, and that won't improve right away. Not only does our staff have to abide by the guidelines to quarantine if they've been exposed, but they're also facing unprecedented family issues. Those with children in school need time off to find daycare when schools are closed, and we have to accept that some might not be able to do so and may need to take a leave. These are unprecedented times, and we're all doing the best we can."

"There's also the staff that comes to work but are too scared to do their jobs," Greg pointed out. "As the head of HR, what are you doing about that?"

"Ah, yes. You're talking about Kristy, I take it. Kristy's response wasn't unusual, given her circumstances. But that's precisely why we attempted to address any such issues from the onset. I assure you that Kristy didn't expect her response or her fear. Those were involuntary, Greg. And if I can add, it's precisely what involuntary brandslaughter is about, finding areas where we might be out of brand integrity now or in the future and addressing them before they produce undesired consequences. Kristy is a good nurse—I think you know that. It's a shame that we weren't able to keep her."

"Are you insinuating that it's *my* fault?" Greg asked with exasperation.

"I don't know if it is or if it isn't, Greg. But I do believe that it might have been an issue that could have been avoided," Vivian remarked.

"How could I have possibly known she was pregnant? How could I have known she was scared?"

"ABI, Greg. That's what it's for. Survey your staff and let them tell you about potential issues and how they are being affected. Take the time to read our weekly brand integrity audit. I do, and I learn something each and every week."

"Okay, so what if I do? What if I read it and learn something? It seems to me that there's nothing I can do. I can only do the best with what I've been given, whether it's staff, money, or other resources," Greg complained.

"Sometimes, Greg, what's needed is understanding. Perhaps a word of support or encouragement. Recognizing that we're all human and in this together. A promise that they can come to you without fear ..."

"I get it. You think my staff is scared of me," he interjected.

"I didn't say that. But is it possible that they might not feel like they're being heard or supported? Maybe they don't feel you are approachable right now? I don't know the answers, but I do know that, as leaders, it is our responsibility to discover the questions and then we can work together to find the answers that produce the best outcomes—even if that means we have to take a good hard look at ourselves, Greg."

"Start here," she added, handing him a copy of their initial audit of brand integrity. "I can help you develop a survey for your staff if you'd like. I think you have to admit that being reactive isn't working. Let's give 'Illumination' a try," she suggested.

"And then what?" Greg asked, still doubting the process but knowing that he'd have to go along to prove her wrong.

"It's a three-step process, Greg. We can't shove our problems under the rug and hope that sight unseen, they'll go away. We saw how that ended with Kristy. Problems that fester grow until we lose control. Look at it this way, we can't treat an illness unless we don't know about, right?"

"Of course."

"ABI isn't much different than medicine, Greg. Find out what's wrong or what's at risk, face that it could be or is a problem, follow it and then create a plan to fix it," Vivian smiled, thinking that, for the first time, she thought she caught a glimpse of acceptance in the doctor's eyes.

chapter seven

"You need a break."

The suggestion came from Corrine, Greg's wife, who was worried about the long hours he was putting in at the hospital and the stress that he was bringing home with him.

"I can't, Corrine. Nobody can. There is a temporary stop to all requests for time off, except for emergencies. I can't take a day off if my staff can't. How would that look?"

"How would it look if you succumb to exhaustion, Greg? You can only do so much," she countered.

"When this is over, I will take a break, I promise. Just not now," Greg said.

Unfortunately, no one knew when "this" would be over. The schools were closed, and all but what were referred to as "essential" workers had been given notices of layoffs or were working from home. Lockdowns were the norm, delegating the public to isolation in their homes, except for what was again deemed "essential" errands or trips.

The only place groups of people could be found were in department and grocery stores and in the lines of people waiting to be tested for the virus. Restaurants, theaters, and small shops were, for the most part, closed to the public. And if anyone took a walk through Reliance Hospital, they might assume the hospital was off limits as well. The corridors were empty and there were more vacant than occupied parking spaces in the lots.

But if one took a walk into the bowels of the hospital, they'd find a handful of wards bustling with activity. The units designated for caring for pandemic victims were at high occupancy, and concern about a lack of available beds for that population closed another unit in preparation for an increase in patients needing inpatient care. Census numbers for the cardiac and labor and delivery units were also consistent, proving that heart attacks and births operate on their own timetable.

Still, there were empty wings—medical and surgical units were noticeably empty, as were the hospital's outpatient and rehab centers, physician offices, and lab testing department.

The low numbers troubled Phillip. The hospital's staff and physical structure were based on providing these services, and without them, they had experienced a significant loss in revenue—revenue that was instrumental in meeting payroll and paying vendors. A significant financial shortfall would limit their ability to meet their contractual obligations and provide the standard of care and services that had earned Reliance multiple healthcare awards.

It was for that reason that Phillip called an administrative meeting of all department heads. It was time to disclose their financial outlook and, to his disappointment, make necessary budget cuts.

Greg took a seat next to Dr. Barrett, who ran Reliance's cardiac surgery department. Along with the hospital's other department heads, they listened as Phillip shared that the hospital had experienced a 40 percent drop in revenue, which was unprecedented in its history.

"This is a loss we simply cannot absorb," he explained. "Therefore, we will immediately begin to make cuts wherever we can. Unfortunately, that means that there will be staff furloughs, and, in some cases, departments may be combined or temporarily closed. I understand that this will be difficult for all of us, but it is a necessary measure that cannot be avoided."

"Are you kidding me?" Dr. Hicks asked Dr. Barrett.

"He looks dead serious to me," Dr. Barrett answered. "But if it helps, I think our departments will escape the brunt of it."

"I hope you're right. I have to tell you, I didn't see this coming, pandemic or no pandemic. I mean, just a couple months ago, Reliance was growing at a rapid pace. Look how many outpatient clinics they opened in the last year alone!" Greg whispered.

"I know, crazy, isn't it," Dr. Barrett agreed. "Just goes to show that sometimes everything isn't in our control. I have to tell myself that in the operating room from time to time."

"Yeah, I know what you mean. But it's a shame. We have some outstanding employees who don't deserve this, that's for sure.

This pandemic just keeps throwing us curves. What'll it be next?" Greg asked.

With a shrug of his shoulders, Dr. Barrett turned his attention to the hospital's Chief Financial Officer, who was explaining that, while the details were in the preliminary stages, they would be presenting their initial recommendations to the board of directors later that day.

"We will keep you abreast of the details as they become clear," he said. "In the meantime, this information is intended to help you prepare by identifying areas where we can all make voluntary, less crucial, cuts. We thought it was necessary to share our circumstances with you because your input can help us identify ways to reduce our shortfall, while maintaining the quality of services we offer. As we've learned in the years we've been implementing ABI, we've found a critical issue. We might not like it, but we have to face it, follow it and work as a team to fix it."

Walking out of the president's conference room, Dr. Hicks decided to step outside for a breath of fresh air before returning to his department. It was a warm spring day, the kind of day that made everything look bright, sunny, and promising.

Mother Nature obviously doesn't know there's a pandemic, he thought sarcastically. *Otherwise, she'd be at risk of being out of a job, too.*

As he strolled along the tulips and daffodils that lined the walkway, he looked forward to the end of his shift when he could go home and enjoy the unusually warm weather. He pulled out his phone to tell Corrine not to cook—he'd throw something on the grill—but before he could make the call, his attention was diverted.

Car keys in hand, a nurse who had just gotten off work approached a man who was sitting on the sidewalk with his head in his hands.

"Sir, are you okay?" she asked.

"Yes," he answered. "Wait no, I'm not," he corrected in a shaky voice that was on the edge of tears.

"What's wrong? Do you need medical help?" the nurse asked, looking up and catching Dr. Hicks's eyes.

"Yes … uh, no. It's not me; it's my wife," he cried.

"What's wrong? Where is your wife?" the nurse prodded, now with urgency in her voice.

"She's in the hospital. She's having our baby," he answered.

"Sir, you seem upset. Can I do something to help you?" she continued the inquisition.

"They won't let me in. Can you let me in?" he pleaded with his words and his eyes.

Dr. Hicks stepped in and learned that the man had allergies. Unfortunately, some of his symptoms mimicked those of the virus, and without a negative test, the rules said that he couldn't enter the hospital. He'd been sitting outside for several hours, receiving occasional updates from his wife's nurse—the last of which indicated that she was being prepped for delivery.

"This is our first baby—we've been trying for years. And now I can't be there with her."

The nurse looked at Dr. Hicks for direction that didn't come.

"I wish there was something I could …" she said, before an idea hit her.

"Wait! Do you have a phone on you?" she asked.

"Uh, yes, the nurse said she'd call and let me know when the baby is born."

"I think we can do better than that," she replied, taking her phone out of her purse. "What's your name?"

"Jason—Jason Sullivan," he answered.

After entering his name and phone number in her phone, the nurse said, "Okay, got it. My name is Sherry. I want you to wait right here. When your phone rings, answer it. It'll be me."

Greg took in the scene and saw a nervous father. He had been one at one time, too. But he had been an excited nervous father. He realized that this man and his wife should have been experiencing one of the happiest moments of their life together, yet they were each alone, frightened, and upset. And it was no fault of their own.

Damn pandemic, he thought. A pang of sympathy hit him, and he pulled out his phone and alerted his staff that he'd be there soon — he was assisting in the birth of a child.

Then he helped the man to his feet and walked with him to a nearby bench and waited for his phone to ring.

The call came ten minutes later, and the face of the nurse who had just been outside with them sprang onto the screen.

"I'm here with your wife," she said. "And she's getting ready to push. I'm going to hold the phone and video this so you can see your wife and she can see and hear you. Your job, Jason, is to coach her through this, just like you would if you were by her side."

Greg watched Jason's eyes light up.

"Okay! Hon, are you ready? Listen to me, okay, just like we did in the classes."

"Okay, Jase. Honey, I am so glad you're here," she sighed.

"Me, too, babe. Me, too," he managed to say as a female voice instructed his wife to push.

Greg listened, reassuring Jason that he was doing great. "Only a few more pushes, and you'll be a dad," he said. "Don't worry. Everything's going great. Talk her through it—you're almost there."

A few minutes later, Greg was the first one to congratulate the new father on the birth of their first child—a healthy baby girl. As the new parents doted on her and shared their joy virtually, Greg knew he had done the right thing by staying with Jason. It was the least he could do.

It was one of those heartwarming moments that didn't happen often—the kind that warranted sharing, which was what Greg did when he returned to his department. As his staff commended him, he corrected them—the person who deserved the recognition was Sherry, a nurse he had never met before. She had clocked out, and like everyone else, had already put in a long, stressful day. But she didn't think twice when someone was in need.

Because of her, two parents got to experience the birth of their first child together. Because of her, what could have potentially been a devastating experience was turned into a positive and happy celebration.

"I can't take the credit," he explained. "Sherry went out of her way. She was the one who stopped, found out what the problem was, and …"

Realizing what he had just stopped, Greg stopped abruptly.

Face it, follow it, fix it … he thought, and turned his head to a box on the wall, labeled simply, 'Outstanding Brand Integrity NOMINATIONS.'

It was at that moment that he truly got it. Nothing Sherry had done was in her job description. In fact, she wasn't even on the clock anymore. But she was everything that Reliance was about — everything Reliance prided itself on.

Compassionate care … the kindest touch. To some, they were merely words on their mission statement. But to people like Sherry, they were at the heart of everything they did. She lived their brand — no, she *was* the embodiment of their brand. And to Greg Hicks, she deserved to be recognized for it.

It's a good thing she was still here, he thought, before realizing that if the budget cuts had already been imposed, there was a strong possibility that she, or others like her, would not be there for the people who turned to them in times of need.

Reliance might be facing financial struggles at the moment, but Greg knew the one thing they couldn't afford was to lose good employees, like Sherry. Regardless if the impending cuts would affect his department or not, he made up his mind to ensure that wouldn't happen.

chapter eight

The pandemic made its presence known swiftly and boldly. Some staff had been furloughed, and once thriving departments had now been closed. The physical therapy and rehab centers were dark and empty, and the cafeteria was closed to the public. Flower and plant deliveries had been curtailed, at least for the time being, and the absence of those symbols of well wishes and expressions of cheer gave the hospital an impersonal atmosphere that matched the lack of compassion and interaction being expressed in the public.

People were at war with each other, some fearful, some nonchalant about the pandemic. Social distancing was the norm, but the beliefs on both viewpoints were even farther apart.

But there was an unlikely joining of the minds.

Reliance Hospital was the largest hospital in the county, but not the only one within a 20-mile radius. Both of the hospitals worked directly with the health departments and received their information and guidelines from the same agencies. Because there had been daily updates and frequent press conferences, Phillip was in regular contact with Kenneth Mullen, the other hospital's

CEO. They'd known each other for years and had attended many of the same medical functions. But they kept a professional distance—after all, they were competitors, each seeking growth and higher standards than the other.

At the press conference the day before, Phillip approached Kenneth, asking him how his facility was dealing with the aftermath of the pandemic. As they talked, it became apparent that both executives were facing the same issues, which gave them a common bond and an opportunity to sit down together to seek solutions. No longer were they competing; they saw an opportunity to collaborate and work together to help their communities.

That was why they were sitting down for a joint meeting. Kenneth had indicated that his hospital was experiencing major issues at a greater level than Reliance. Phillip listened as the CEO told him that their revenue shortfall could actually result in permanent changes—even if the pandemic ended soon, it was a dire situation that they might not be able to recover from. And his staff knew it. Nurses, techs, CNAs, physicians, and even support staff were searching for positions elsewhere, in places that might be more financially stable. While they were loyal to the hospital, they had to look out for themselves.

What he heard was concerning. Phillip knew that if their competitor closed its doors, it would put even more stress on Reliance and its staff. When the pandemic ended, they wouldn't have the capacity to absorb a sharp increase in patients, whether that meant hospital beds, equipment, staff, or other resources. A sharp businessman, Phillip knew that if they experienced rapid growth that they could not accommodate, it would jeopardize

Reliance's reputation and employees. And he couldn't let that happen.

For that reason, he offered to help his biggest competitor.

"Ken, I know this is unexpected, but it is sincere. I'd like to help you if I can."

"I don't know how you can be of help. It seems we're both facing the same challenges here, but your hospital is larger. I think you can absorb the effects a little longer than we can, but it's just a matter of time before we'll all have to admit that this isn't looking good," Kenneth said.

"You might be right. But I do know that there are things you *can* do right now, starting today, that will help you retain your employees and earn the confidence of your patients. It's a tool we've been using for years, and we found we had to turn to it from another angle to be proactive during this pandemic."

"What tool is that?" asked the CEO.

"ABI."

"Who's Abby? You're saying you have an employee who has all the answers?"

"No, but wouldn't that be nice! Ken, what I am saying is that we have an audit that leads us to answers from *all* of our employees. It's called the Audit of Brand Integrity, ABI for short," he explained. "I'm not saying it has all the answers, but it was a godsend in helping us foresee potential issues and address them before they had a negative impact on our brand. Like I said, we still have issues, but every week, ABI helps us identify them before they snowball down the hill and become bigger and bigger."

"Okay, I'm interested. Tell me more," Ken said.

"I'll do even better. I had my assistant make copies of everything you need to implement ABI at your facility. It's all right there," he said, pointing to a box of binders on the table. "I think it will help you in preventing brandslaughter, even when it's involuntary and out of your control."

"I didn't think I'd ever say this, Phillip, but thank you for your counsel. I don't know if it'll work, but I'm willing to review the information. You know, I never thought I'd see the day when our competitor would go out of their way to help us in times of trouble," Kenneth said. "Thank you. Really, thank you."

"These are unusual times, aren't they? But as the CEO of Reliance Hospital, I, too, have to live our brand each and every day, and I asked myself not what I should do, but what would be true to our brand. And I came to the conclusion that keeping your hospital open and viable was in the best interests of the community's health and safety. If I chose to look the other way, I'd be out of integrity with what we stand for, Kenneth. I'd be committing what we call brandslaughter in the first degree."

While the two executives were mending once opposing fences, the emergency department was facing a different type of opposition.

"Unit 7 to Reliance, enroute with a male, gunshot victim, wound to the chest. Critical. ETA 5 minutes."

Thirty seconds later, another call came in.

"Unit 2 to Reliance, enroute with a 32-year-old male, gunshot wound to the abdomen. ETA 6 minutes."

"Oh, great," Dr. Hicks muttered. "They won't stop trying to kill each other, even during a pandemic."

Then turning his attention toward prepping for possible casualties, he ordered, "All hands on deck, get moving!"

WOOP, WOOP came the alarm on the intercom. WOOP, WOOP.

The security code that followed alerted all employees that the hospital was on lockdown.

"Okay, everybody. You know the drill. No one is to enter or leave the unit without security clearance!" he advised the ED employees.

The doors to the ambulance entrance flew open, and in rushed a group of paramedics who were quickly pushing an adult male with an open wound to the chest.

"Room Two!" Greg yelled, following directly behind. "When the next unit arrives, put them in Room Eight."

A quick assessment of the wound revealed that time there was no time for extensive testing or taking any other measures. The patient's only hope of living was emergency surgery—and there was no time to waste. Dr. Hicks informed his nurse to alert to the operating team to be ready and STAT.

Across the department, a crowd of policemen and first responders had gathered around room eight. When Dr. Hicks walked in, he could see that the patient was in uniform. He realized instantly that the victim was a police officer.

"He responded to a shots-fired call. Got caught in the crossfire. Greg, you've got to help him. He's one of the best."

Greg Hicks looked over to see that those words came from his brother-in-law, Kevin, who was visibly shaken and worried.

"I'll do what I can," he said and quickly assessed the patient's wounds and vitals.

"How about the other guy? He gonna make it?" someone asked.

"He's headed to surgery. That's all I can tell you," Dr. Hicks replied.

"Well, if you can only save one of them, save Ty, not some no-good gangbanger!"

"I promise to take care of him. We're going to have to call in an off-duty team to operate, and that could take a little longer. Let's stabilize the bleeding first ..."

"Doctor, you better hurry! His blood pressure is dropping," urged a nurse.

At that very second, the monitor's alarm started beeping.

"He's crashing!"

"Call a code! I need everyone available! Everyone else, get out!" Greg yelled.

"You gotta help him! You gotta help him!" Kevin screamed. "Don't let him die, Greg!"

"Get him out of here," Dr. Hicks said, instructing his nurse to get his brother-in-law out of the doorway.

Ten minutes later, they had managed to raise the officer's blood pressure, but his injuries were obviously life threatening. Dr. Hicks had called for another surgical team and followed the stretcher as the patient was quickly transferred to the surgical unit.

"What if they're not here yet?" the nurse asked.

"Just get him in there. If I have to, I'll start surgery without them," he said. "Has anyone called his next of kin?"

"Yes, Tracy just did," she answered.

"Are they on their way?"

"Doctor, they're already here. The officer is Vivian's son."

chapter nine

 Dr. Hicks notified his staff that he would be observing the surgery and to alert him if he was needed. For the time being, that was unlikely, given that the hospital was still on lockdown and would be until law enforcement felt that it was safe to reopen their doors. In the past, there had been attempts to retaliate when an individual was injured or shot, and a cooperative agreement between the medical and law enforcement personnel was designed to ensure everyone's safety and wellbeing.

The galley was empty, with the exception of a couple interns, when Dr. Hicks sat down to observe the officer's surgery. The two surgeons performing the operation had given their orders, and their team bustled to make sure everything was in place.

Shortly after the first incision was made, the head surgeon raised his head toward the galley and looked directly at Greg.

"Nice work, Hicks," he said. "Now, let's hope it holds."

Greg acknowledged his remark with a nod of the head and kept his eye on the patient—a police officer who was a "brother" and buddy of his own brother-in-law, and the son of their Human

Resources Officer. First responders were a tight group, exhibited by the respectably sized group of officers in the waiting room. His thoughts then turned to Vivian, and he felt a pang of personal responsibility for her son's recovery. It was one of the reasons some doctors prefer not to accept friends as patients—it allowed emotions to enter into their professional judgment, something Hicks tried to avoid.

Within the hour, the surgeon announced that they had stopped the bleeding and repaired the damage. But the work was only halfway done. The neurosurgeon was waiting in the wings to take over and start the very delicate process of removing the bullet, which, just as Dr. Hicks had suspected, was lodged precariously close to the patient's spine. This stage would be very deliberate and meticulous; they not only had to determine what damage had been done, but avoiding additional injuries required extreme caution.

It was a good time to take a break and check in with his staff. As he walked down the hall, he spotted a handful of police officers talking outside the waiting room. Peering his head in, he saw Vivian, who was holding hands with her husband. The professional, confident woman that he had known and often admired had been replaced with the face of vulnerable face of a frightened parent. He'd seen the face before, but not on her, and it was so private that he turned his head, feeling like he had intruded on her pain.

With a deep sigh, he said a silent prayer that God would spare this young man, and he wondered if he had made the right decision. It was obvious that the other victim would have certainly died without immediate surgery, and the severity of Ty's injuries weren't as apparent on initial examination. However, the pleas by Kevin and Ty's fellow officers haunted him … but he also knew he'd taken an oath to base his medical decisions not on who people were, but rather on their medical needs. Sure, the pleas stemmed from emotion, and Greg was confident that his brother-in-law knew that Greg did what he had to do in the moment — still, it instilled a seed of doubt in his mind, one that wasn't easily shaken.

He didn't see Vivian until the surgery was over and the patients were both in recovery. The young male was expected to recover, but he had a long road ahead of him, one that would likely pose complications and require long-term care. Ty would be transferred to intensive care, where he would be closely monitored to determine the extent of his injuries. There was a possibility that he would be paralyzed, or at the very least, require rehabilitation in order to be able to walk.

It was a sad outcome for both patients, made even worse by the fact that their injuries didn't have to happen. They were victims, but not of unavoidable accidents.

"Vivian," Greg said as he entered the post-surgical waiting room. "I just want to let you know that I'm sorry and if there is anything I can do …"

"I appreciate it, Greg," she said in a shaky voice. "And thank *you*. I understand you treated Ty in the ED."

"I did. And I observed his surgery. I assure you, they took excellent care of your son. And please, let me know if you need anything, anything at all."

The words sounded empty, but they were heartfelt. And they weren't typical for Greg Hicks. Usually, he was the epitome of professionalism when speaking with patients' families. But this wasn't usual ... to Vivian, her husband, Ty's fellow officers, and Kevin, it was personal.

That reminded him to connect with his brother-in-law. Pulling out his phone, he wrote a short text to Kevin.

"He made it through surgery. I can't say much but wanted you to know."

A reply came quickly.

"Thank God! And I'm sorry, bro. Didn't mean to come down so hard on you. Emotions got the best of me."

"No problem. Talk later," was Greg's reply.

When he returned to his department, he was informed that Security would be stationed inside the department, as well as outside, for the next 24 hours. A crowd of approximately 30 people had congregated near the entrance, demanding to be able to see the younger gunshot victim. In such instances, to protect the patient and the staff, visitors were limited to two members and they must be relatives. However, the pandemic had tightened those restrictions, and now only one visitor was allowed, and that visitor must be a member of the immediate family.

The restrictions were made as an abundance of caution and in conjunction with local law enforcement agencies. The safety and wellbeing of everyone was at stake, and even the slightest risk needed to be marginalized. Instances such as these were not frequent, so when they occurred, staff was naturally uneasy. But still, Dr. Hicks knew that, regardless if the victim was involved in the commission of a crime, he or she had family members and people who loved them. It was likely that they were feeling the same anguish and concern that he saw on Vivian's face earlier.

It was about an hour before his shift was over when he heard the commotion. The crowd had become unruly, demanding to come inside to see their loved one. He heard a woman wailing, stating that it was her grandson and she had a right to see him. A male was very loud and vocal; as he became louder, his tone became threatening, and the walkie talkies became more active, calling for assistance.

The assistance wasn't far, for there were two officers already stationed outside the gunshot victim's hospital room and several other officers were in the waiting room, where they would keep round the clock support for their brother in blue until he was out of intensive care. Armed officers ran through the empty halls and stationed themselves in the emergency department, making sure that the staff and patients just beyond the entrance were safe in the event things got out of control.

A few minutes later, the crowd dispersed, with the exception of a few who were committed to remaining as close as they could be to their wounded relative. And for the first time since the code was alerted earlier that day, Dr. Hicks let his guard down—he needed a breather.

Like many areas in Reliance Hospital, a wall in the break room was dedicated to the institution's mission statement. He had read it a million times. It was the foundation of their brand and the basis of their audit of brand integrity. Every ABI meeting addressed it, and every employee knew it by heart. But today, unlike any other day, when Greg Hicks sat down at the break table and stared at the wall, it was like seeing the words for the first time.

To provide the highest quality care in the safest environment,

To deliver compassionate care with the kindest touch,

Making health and wellness a priority available to everyone who walks through our doors.

He no sooner got past the second line, compassionate care with the kindest touch, that the weight of his emotions became too much to bear. His face in his hands, he placed his elbows on the table and began to sob. The tears were for a world where innocent people were hurt, for children who were struck with life-threatening illnesses, for parents who worried and grieved, and for himself and people like him who were charged with saving lives but sometimes fell short … and for a community riddled with fear that they would be the next victim of an undiscriminating pandemic.

That's how one of the technicians found him when they walked into the room. Immediately, she turned around and whispered to the head nurse, "Hey, Dr. Hicks is in the break room, and I'm not sure, but I think he's *crying.*"

Standing in the doorway, the nurse looked at their department head—a man who was always assured, strong and steady, a doctor who took pride in being a true professional who was able to separate his emotions from his responsibilities.

But she didn't see Dr. Hicks—she saw Greg, a human being with feelings, and one who had just had one hell of a bad day. Ever so quietly, she walked to him and without saying a word, sat in the chair beside him and reached out her gloved hand to hold his, offering him support through the compassion of her presence and the kindest touch.

The two sat silently, each realizing that there would always be unexpected things that would be outside of their control, but when you tried to pretend they didn't exist, they had a way of building up inside until, finally, the dam had to break.

chapter ten

 Duncan led the audit of brand integrity meeting in Vivian's stead, making sure she could invest her time and energy toward helping her son recover from his injuries.

In opening the meeting, he provided the committee with an update on Ty's condition.

"The officer is in good spirits, despite the long road ahead of him. We wish him well as he undergoes physical therapy to regain his strength and have made it known to his family that they have our support and best wishes on the path ahead," he announced.

From there, Duncan gave the results of their most recent brand integrity audit—a mini audit that gave them insight into areas where they were performing well, as well as areas that needed attention and/or correction.

They had gotten a handle on personal protection equipment, and their supplies of masks, gloves, sanitizer, and gowns was no longer a critical issue. In the rare event that there was a noticeable drop in supplies, procedures had been implemented to find the reason and measures were taken to avoid any recurrence.

Staff call offs had stabilized, for the most part, but that was one area that would fluctuate, depending on many factors, including exposure to the virus and spikes in community numbers testing positive for the virus. The medical staff knew that spikes and falls in the number of cases among hospital personnel would closely mirror those in the community. Enough time had passed that they had been able to recruit and train additional employees who could be called in on an as-needed basis, which relieved the fear of dire staff shortages due to the pandemic.

Yes, staff had been furloughed, and entire departments had been closed so the administration and personnel could focus on the most pressing medical needs among the public. The unemployment numbers were unfortunate, but in this case, they had been deemed necessary to fund vital areas of the hospital.

Then Duncan asked if there were any new issues that had been brought to anyone's attention. For the first time since the pandemic started, the room was silent.

Then, Dr. Hicks cleared his throat.

"I'd like to address an issue if I may," he said.

"Please proceed," Duncan nodded.

"As most of you know, I have voiced my skepticism over the audit of brand integrity in the past. However, I have been required to follow the guidelines that are in place, so I can also see that it has benefits. I recognize now that by identifying potential problems early on, we can control the damage they might cause. In fact, in some cases, we can avoid that damage altogether … and I think Phillip, Vivian, and Duncan have done a good job of apprising us of those issues and finding the best solution, given the circumstances and resources available."

"Thank you," Phillip said.

"You're welcome. But I'm not done. You see, it has come to my attention that we are falling short in one area—one that I believe has the capability of destroying not only our brand, but our entire reputation. And I'll even go so far as to say that it has the power to severely damage staff morale and cause burnout hospital wide," Dr. Hicks stated.

"What is that?" Duncan asked, pen in hand.

"Due to pandemic guidelines, we cannot live by our mission statement—and our mission statement is the foundation of everything we do and everything we are. Yes, we do provide quality care in the safest environment, given our present circumstances, and we do not turn anyone in need of medical attention away. But three-letter agencies have tied our hands and actually *prohibited* us from fulfilling our mission to offer *compassionate* care with the *kindest* touch. Patients, family members, and even fellow staff members don't receive compassion anymore. How can they? We are masked faces, covered from head to toe to protect us from their germs! To the naked eye, it looks like we're treating them like lepers! Sure, we can try to make up for it with a smile, but when's the last time anyone could see a smile? They're covered by the masks that we're forced to wear when we're within proximity of anyone— anyone at all! And how about the kindest touch—the one thing that heals and comforts more than medicine? We can't touch anyone, at least not without making sure every inch of our skin is covered. And before you say anything, I know that's not within our control—we have to follow guidelines. But I pose a question to you, and it's one that I hope you think long and hard about: What are the ramifications when we, as medical personnel and caregivers, are the ones in need of that compassion, and that kind touch? How many of us will reach our limit as the stress without those heartfelt signs of support and care continues to climb? It has already affected my team, and I admit that it has impacted me, as well. How long will it be before our morale declines even more than it already has? How much more can we give when we are deprived of the one thing that called us to our professions in the first place—being able to express our concern, care, understanding, and gratitude with those we treat and work with? There are times when words fall short and our patients and team members need just what we promise to provide, but we are failing to deliver—compassion and a kind *touch*. As it is, we are offering medical care in a sterile environment, a cold, clinical environment with a bedside manner that is as sterile as the facility."

Greg's questions didn't require an answer. They were a plea, asking for a solution, one that wasn't immediately forthcoming.

"I just want to say that I believe we are on the brink of a major problem, and if it hasn't already affected everyone here at Reliance, I predict it will. People are more than potential virus carriers—they are human. They have feelings and emotions; and if we are only allowed to address their medical issues, we are neglecting the very reason we are here. Long-term neglect doesn't save lives, and it won't save Reliance Hospital. It will kill it," Dr. Hicks said.

"Greg, you've just defined brandslaughter in the first degree. And as you know, that's what ABI is for, even when potential brandslaughter is not due to our actions, but state and federal medical policies and protocols," Duncan replied. "And I want to thank you for bringing these issues to our attention. If we don't know about them, we cannot face them, follow them, or fix them."

"Face it, because it's happening," Greg retorted. "My question is, how are you going to fix it?"

"As you know, there is nothing we can do about the PPE—it's for everyone's health and safety. If we violated that policy, we'd lose our accreditation, and then where would we be? Social distancing is also an issue, and I think that is an area we *can* look into when it comes to interacting with our peers. Obviously, there is tension, and I think you're right—ignoring it won't make it go away. Are you willing to chair a subcommittee to address this shortcoming and help us ascertain the best way to fulfill our mission statement without violating pandemic protocols?"

"Who, *me?*" Greg asked in surprise,

"Yes," Phil replied. "It seems to me that you have a very good grasp of the problem and are, therefore, in a position to enlighten others and find the best solution to it."

Dr. Hicks's chest heaved as he let out a deep sigh before responding.

"I should've seen this coming," he said. "But okay, I'll do it. I've lost a good nurse over these concerns, and I've seen what happens when we remove compassion and human-to-human interaction and touch with our patients and family members. It's not good for us, it's not good for our patients, and it's not good for society. So, yes, I'll do it."

"Okay, meet with Duncan after the meeting, and he'll help you get started. And, again, thank you for bringing this to our attention. I believe you've revealed a critical issue and have my full support moving forward," Phil said.

The remainder of the meeting consisted of addressing patient complaints that were made to the hospital liaison and a few comments that staff members had placed in suggestion boxes that were strategically placed throughout campus. For the most part, they were routine and simply needed approval before moving forward with resolving the issues and addressing the concerns. In short time, the meeting was adjourned, and instead of leaving the meeting immediately, as he always did, Greg waited for Duncan to gather his papers.

He had faced the problems and laid them out on the table. As a doctor, he was well aware of what could happen when problems were ignored. Walking away while those problems were still a threat would be committing malpractice, jeopardizing the hospital's mission and violating his professional code of ethics. Having faced the fact that the hospital, its patients, and the careers of Reliance's staff were at stake, he accepted that, like it or not, he must play a role in fixing it.

To do otherwise, would make him complicit in the "crime" of brandslaughter.

chapter eleven

 "How is EMS coping with all of the virus guidelines?" Greg asked his brother-in-law, Kevin.

"The guidelines are easy—they're written out in black and white, and as far as I can tell, they're not optional. I think our biggest problems are the fear and stress that the pandemic is leaving in its trail," Kevin said.

"On behalf of both the patients and medical staff," Greg added. "I brought this up in a meeting, and wouldn't you know, it landed me another committee assignment."

"Oh, yeah? Making more work for yourself, are you?" laughed Kevin. "So, what's the new gig?"

"Well, it's no secret that I've been frustrated by the requirements handed down from both the three-letter agencies and our administration. Kevin, everyone has a breaking point, and I've watched as several highly professional members of my department reached theirs. Truth be told, I haven't been exempt from feeling overwhelmed and frustrated. Hell, I've watched a virus hijack the way we perform our duties. There's no compassion, or if there is, we are too damn scared to show it. We've become a bunch of faceless, masked people, all living in our own germ-free little bubbles, and it's affecting us and our patients."

"That's for sure," Kevin sighed. "But what can we do about it?"

"I guess that's what I have to figure out. Looks like I'm chairing a committee to figure out how to help our patients and staff interact humanely in a way that people need—you know, showing care, concern, and even a friendly face. And that's just half of it. There's a stress factor that we need to figure out how to reduce, as well," Greg said.

"Stress for who? Medical staff or the patients?"

"Ah, good question. I'm going to go out on a limb here and say both."

"Well, when you have the answers, let me know, will ya? It's been a long year already, and it's looking like it's not going to get any better," Kevin stated. "Until then, I'm going to kick back and have a cold one while you finish grilling those burgers."

Greg used that same casual tone in his committee's first meeting. Never having been an executive type, he wasn't fond of meetings. For that reason, he preferred a more casual atmosphere, which he truly felt was more conducive when seeking new perspectives, insights, and solutions. The Illuminate Model of face, follow, and fix was something he found he agreed with, and he hoped by being encouraging and supporting any and all ideas, they could find the fix to pandemic's effects.

"You are here today because you've been recommended by your supervisor who believes you can contribute real value to our staff. We all know the pandemic has taken a toll on our hospital and its patients. While that toll couldn't be prevented in its entirety, we find ourselves in a unique situation where we need to address those effects before they do any further damage. As you know, staff morale is down and stress is up—for both staff and patients. Our mission is to find ways to improve morale, reduce stress, and return the compassionate care we're known for, despite the guidelines and restrictions that have been imposed on us," he announced.

"What do you suggest?" asked a charge nurse.

"I'm open to any and all ideas. Let's take some time to hash out the issues, and then we'll get to work on ways we can address them. I do want you to know that we have the full support of administration, so this isn't one of those projects that will fall to the wayside. In fact, they're open to spending money if necessary to implement any suggestions that sound promising," Greg said.

An hour later, they were all in agreement that patients and their families deserved a more personal relationship with the medical professionals they entrusted. And they were unanimous in pointing out that there was little expression of joy or happiness in their interactions.

"Now, what do we do about it? I want everyone to feel free to speak up. No idea is too small or too large at this point. As a group, let's really explore our alternatives," Greg suggested.

"I think you're right, Dr. Hicks. When it comes to relationships with patients, what is their biggest complaint? I think it's that they don't like their 'bedside manner.' We've heard that many times, which really makes me think it's very important that patients and family members receive a sign of kindness, even a smile. It can go a long way, especially in trying times. I used to tell my staff to make sure they smile when they encounter the public on hospital grounds," the chief security officer said. "But now nobody knows if we're smiling or not."

"That's exactly my point. How can patients 'see' your smile, a nurse's kindness, or a doctor's compassion when we're masked every minute of the day?" asked Dr. Hicks.

"Right! I guess the only way to do that would be if they can see us smile through our eyes," interjected Jose', who oversaw the physical therapy department. "These aren't issues with virtual appointments and employees in other industries—hell, in a zoom meeting, you can see everything from smiles to boxer shorts," he laughed.

"Wait a minute! I think you're onto something," Greg exclaimed. "Our eyes *can* see a smile, even if it's masked! Hear me out ... in a zoom meeting or virtual appointment, cameras show our faces, and we know that's safe. We smile with our mouths, but we also see smiles with our eyes. What if we used our existing technology to *show* patients our full unmasked, smiling faces?"

"I'm not sure I'm following you, Dr. Hicks," said Jose'.

"Okay, I'm thinking out loud, so bear with me. Every patient room in the hospital is equipped with a monitor that provides short presentations about health issues—in October, we promote breast cancer awareness. There's also heart health, men's health, and even information on flu and virus prevention. What if those monitors also included a 'Meet Your Medical Team' presentation?"

"Oh, interesting idea—that'd be a way to let them see us without a mask! I like it!"

"Wait a second! What if it showed us with the mask *and* without the mask? Maybe a video that shows us wearing the mask and pulling it down to reveal our smile. The big reveal would show the smile they could only see in our eyes before!" Greg said with excitement.

"Yes! It's easy, and like you said, we already have the technology to do it. We just need to work with marketing to create the video streams and IT to upload them," added the charge nurse.

"Okay, let's split up—do I have two volunteers to put the proposal together and work with marketing to make it happen?" Dr. Hicks asked. "Then another group can be focused on reducing stress. Jose', I want you to head up that team."

"Okay, do you have any ideas to get us started?" he asked. "Exercise is a great stress and anxiety reducer, and so is meditation. But that's not realistic when you're on duty, so this is going to be a tough one."

"I suggest you do some research to see what's new and what other hospitals are doing for their staff. Don't rule anything out. If it has potential, let's take a look at it," said Greg.

One week later, the marketing department wowed Greg with their video campaign, which they referred to as "smEYEles." The smile channel would run as the screensaver in all patient rooms, even in the emergency department. The proposal was met with unanimous approval—it was cost effective, and it checked many of the ABI boxes, providing a solution that supported their mission and their brand.

"Good work, Greg," Vivian voiced her support. "We'll get started on this right away. Now, what's the status on stress reduction? Making any headway there?"

"I'm glad you asked. Jose' has been working on that with Miranda, our chief psychologist, and they've left no stone unturned. They're pulling together a lot of information about one of the most innovative products in the industry. While the manufacturer would typically send a representative to demonstrate the product in person, we can't do that during pandemic. So, we'll be setting up an interactive virtual demonstration so we can all see it for ourselves. It's new on the market, groundbreaking, if you will. I'm excited to see if it's as impressive as Jose' and Miranda believe it is."

"It sounds interesting. What is it?" asked Phil.

"It's called a Rejuvenation Station™, and God knows we could all use some rejuvenation every once in a while. I'll send you the login for the virtual demonstration as soon as it's all coordinated. I'd like everyone to participate if you can. If Jose' and Miranda are right, this just might be something to be excited about."

chapter twelve

 "As you can see, the rejuvenation station™ was designed to support the mental, emotional, and physical wellbeing of its users. I think we can all agree that there has never been a time when it is needed more than now. The pandemic has brought us more than a virus, but also an increased amount of stress, anxiety, and, yes, an enormous amount of uncertainty and fear," the saleswoman said during the live video presentation.

"Of course, we all need to destress and decompress at times. This is particularly true for caretakers and medical professionals, who often treat patients with emergency or life-threatening conditions. We understand the unique needs and environment of the medical community, which is why the rejuvenation station™ was designed specifically for them," she continued.

The monitor then revealed the rejuvenation station™, which was a booth that looked like it belonged in a spa, rather than in a hospital. The viewers were then led through a virtual demonstration, experiencing its features alongside the user. Each station offers six different videos and correlating soothing or uplifting music, providing a surround sound experience that engaged all the senses.

"Each video is one to three minutes in length, providing a respite from the sights and sounds of the hospital while *within* the hospital," she explained. "It's an opportunity to get away from the hustle and bustle and surround your staff with a calm, stress-free state of mind."

"Does it work?" one of the board members asked. "Is there any data reflecting the benefits or results?"

"Thank you for that question. The rejuvenation stations™ have been tested, and they have been installed in hospitals across the nation. The results have been more than positive. Before and after they experience their 'journey', they indicate on the touchscreen how they are feeling. The data is collected, and it has revealed a noticeable reduction in stress and anxiety after experiencing just one video. Medically, users have had a significant decrease in blood pressure and heart rate between the time they enter and exit the station. Survey results have consistently stated that the rejuvenation stations™ have quickly become popular. They are especially in demand during high-stress situations—so much so that some hospitals have invested in not just one, but two rejuvenation stations in their emergency departments to make sure all personnel have an opportunity to benefit from them throughout the day. I invite you to visit our website, where you can read reviews, testimonials, and news reports and see the results of surveys conducted at multiple hospitals. Oh, and now they are available in a kiosk form so they can easily be moved from area to area."

The demonstration and question and answer session following it lasted just under one hour, and the more they heard, the more interested the hospital staff became. As the questions steered toward logistics, it became apparent that interest had shifted from should we do this to "how do we make this happen?"

"How much space would we need to dedicate to each station?"

"What utilities and technology will we need to operate it?"

"Does it require routine maintenance?"

And finally, "If we purchase a station today, when could we expect delivery?"

After the meeting, Phil addressed the team.

"Do we need to talk about it, or should we go ahead and get a vote?"

"I say let's vote and see where we stand. We can discuss from there, if we need to," Dr. Hicks suggested.

The vote was unanimous in favor of investing in a rejuvenation station™. The CFO was asked to identify a budget line item to fund the purchase with and get the ball rolling, assuring them that the purchase order would be pushed through the system to avoid any delays.

A few weeks later, Reliance Hospital received its first rejuvenation station™. In the end, they had decided to purchase the portable kiosk version, which would be placed in the emergency department break room.

The central desk was abuzz with anticipation, and staff were claiming their place in line. Before long, they were taking dibs on who would be the first to give it a trial run. It was all in fun, but secretly, every team member hoped that when the time came, it would be them.

The time came the very next day. And when push came to shove, staff forgot about who had dibs and unanimously agreed to give Dr. Hicks the honors of being the first one to use the station, which they quickly nicknamed the RS Go!, an appropriate name because it was able to easily go to wherever they needed it.

"You go, Doctor! We think you should be the first one to check out our new RS Go!"

So he did. Thus far, it had been a slow, even calm, day. They hadn't had a single pandemic patient that morning, and the emergencies were mild according to medical standards. They'd treated a sprained ankle, admitted a middle-aged man who was experiencing AFIB and seen an infant who had a fever, another condition that required inpatient monitoring. A young man had cut his arm at a construction site, requiring six stitches, a tetanus shot, and antibiotics, but nothing too stressful. As Dr. Hicks often said, it was routine.

A group had gathered around the rejuvenation station™ when the time came. Dr. Hicks sat down before it, put on the noise canceling headset, and faced a screen with six choices. Eyeing them, he opted for a video that had clear blue skies topping a body of water, its waves showing the miracle of nature when wind and water meets rocks. While the beautiful visual filled the monitor, the headphones delivered calm, soothing music, providing him with an experience that put him worlds away from the hospital.

Forgetting where he was, he was mesmerized by how quickly he was totally immersed in the experience.

"So how was it?" the charge nursed asked when he stepped out.

"Amazing, really. I was only there for a couple minutes, but it was enough to make me feel like I'd taken a long break!" he answered.

The rest of the day, they took turns, giving everyone an opportunity to use their new RS Go, even the department secretary, housekeeping, and security. Administration personnel came down, also curious about the new station and how it would benefit staff. Their comments were all favorable: "That was so cool!" "I feel like somebody just talked me down and gave me a mental massage," and "I think I'm going to be a frequent flyer. I'd come to work *just* for this respite!"

The rejuvenation station™ quickly became the solution for whatever ailed them. If someone was snippy and short-tempered, they'd be suggested to "Take one," meaning take a break and watch one video. Sometimes when stress levels were higher, they'd be told to take two—two videos were called for in those situations.

They found it was fun, it was relaxing, and it worked. Not only did the station help them deal with situations, but it also helped with their emotions. Staff communicated better, and cooperation levels increased as stress levels decreased.

Four days later, the circumstances were different. The call came in from EMS at 8:04 a.m.—a head-on collision had resulted in a three-car accident with five victims, three of which were teens. Adrenalin was running high as everyone rushed into position, preparing to receive the injured.

Two hours later, one victim had been sent to orthopedics to determine how to treat a fractured leg, and another was in the operating room with a punctured lung and ruptured spleen. One of the teens had been transferred by medical helicopter to another hospital for neurological injuries that likely would need surgery. They were the lucky ones.

Two of the teenagers had not survived. One had perished at the scene, and the other, a 16-year-old girl had internal injuries and went into cardiac arrest before they could get a CT scan. After calling a code, Greg and a team full of doctors and nurses worked for 27 minutes to revive her to no avail.

Finally, Greg called it. Time of death: 9:01 a.m.

"Not yet," argued Marc, a pediatrician who'd answered the code. "Let's give it five more minutes!" he said with a winded voice, while refusing to stop chest compressions.

Knowing that arguing wouldn't make a difference in these circumstances, Dr. Hicks stood to the side and allowed him to continue. Silently, he watched the clock as the room became oddly quiet, given the number of people in it. Exactly five minutes later, Dr. Hicks quietly said, "Time of death: 9:06 a.m."

And then he watched as his respected peer succumbed to the emotions and put his head and his hands and cried.

"Take two, Marc," he said. "I'll talk to her family."

"Doctor, they're outside—they've been exposed and are supposed to be under quarantine," offered a technician.

"I wish that was the reason they'd always remember this day ... but not for this. Not for this," he said, shaking his head as he walked away, thinking it was a shame that a pandemic would be preferred to anything at all, but knowing that, in this instance, it was.

As he often did when they were together, he shared the impact of that tragedy and others with Kevin.

"It's tough, you know. We never want someone to die on our watch, especially not kids. You take that home with you, and it takes a helluva long time to get past it," Greg sighed.

"Yeah, I know. You think it's rough on us? Just imagine their parents. That's a parent's worst nightmare, for sure. I've seen mothers who are in such a panic over an injured kid that they should also receive treatment, even if their child just fell off their bike and need a few stitches," his brother-in-law said.

"Don't I know it. It's not my favorite thing to tell a mom or dad that their child needs to be admitted to the hospital. It's like I can instantly see the fear in their eyes and their stress levels spike," he said.

"Yeah, it's too bad there isn't a rejuvenation station™ for parents, huh?" Kevin said.

"I agree, though it's probably not feasible. Most kids are resilient and recover pretty quickly. They don't have long-term admissions that would justify the expense of giving their parents a dedicated RS Go!, at least not in my opinion," said Greg.

"Except in the NICU," Kevin added.

"The NICU … you know, you're right. Why didn't I think of that?"

"Think of what?" asked Kevin.

"Well, the rejuvenation station™ has become such a hit that people have been asking the hospital to get more. Turns out, we just got word last week that we've received a sizeable donation to our foundation specifically for frontline pandemic workers. It's enough to cover the cost of another portable station, and Phil told me to submit a proposal, but I couldn't figure out where it would be put to best use. But the NICU is perfect, and it would allow us to let families and parents benefit from it, as well. We all know that NICU families are stressed to the limit. Hours turn into days, days into weeks, sometimes months … I can't imagine what it takes to get through it. A rejuvenation station™ could help."

"Especially now with the pandemic and all. I've heard that they've got to go the extra mile to make sure they're not exposed to the virus before getting to see their babies. They could probably use some stress relief, don't you think?"

"We all can, Kevin. I have to admit that I can't wait for the day when everything returns to normal,"

"Whatever that is," Kevin wisely replied.

chapter thirteen

 It was more than a year since Reliance Hospital admitted its first pandemic afflicted patient that there was a return to normal, or at least something resembling it.

A lot had happened in that time. The hospital had reorganized and restructured its departments and services, sometimes out of necessity and sometimes to make sure it was following protocols established by medical associations and governmental agencies. In response, staff had been reduced, with some employees being furloughed and others being reassigned. While it was always difficult to let go of loyal, experienced personnel, it was a necessary measure they had to take in order to address their financial shortfall.

A year before, no one would have predicted these changes. No one would have known what the fallout of a pandemic would look like, or the best way to respond. And now, they still didn't know if everything they had done was right, but they did know that it was better than doing nothing at all.

They owed it to the community to be fiscally sound. They owed it to patients, visitors, vendors, and staff to provide as safe and sterile an environment as possible. The public and all employees deserved to know that, pandemic or not, Reliance was vigilant in addressing their needs and concerns and would remain committed to providing quality healthcare for years to come.

But it hadn't been easy. Far from it. They had to utilize all of their resources, admit their weaknesses, and discover previously hidden strengths. Priorities had to change, sometimes swiftly and drastically, but change they did. A year earlier, no one would have dreamed that their CEO would be helping another hospital in their community address their challenges. A year before, the two CEOs had never participated in a joint press conference. Yet, today, those press conferences had become routine—at first daily and then weekly events.

Today would be their last one. The virus numbers had dropped to the point that frequent radio, television, and newspaper updates were no longer necessary. While there still was a need to wear a mask within the hospital, Reliance was reopening its doors. Their fitness center would return to regular hours. Elective surgeries would be allowed once again, and outpatient rehab and therapy departments would be fully staffed.

Yes, things were changing, but there were some things that came out of the pandemic that would not change.

The SmEYEles campaign was one of them. No one had anticipated just what a hit that idea had become. Patients enjoyed watching the "unmasking" of department staff, and truth be told, the staff had a lot of fun creating the videos; it was a bonding experience to serve the patients in this way. Some got very creative, building up the anticipation of their unmasking, while others had competitions over whose smile was the best. One individual even made his unmasking a game of peek-a-boo, asking the marketing department to edit his video for his big reveal, which started with his hands over his eyes and ended with the caption "Peekaboo! I see you!" which made both children and adults giggle in delight.

The rejuvenation stations had also become a much-used daily fixture. An unexpected, but well received, benefit was that cooperation had increased, while absenteeism and stress levels had decreased. In the NICU, anxious and worried parents praised the hospital for providing them, as well as their babies' caretakers, with an opportunity to enjoy a few minutes of respite, serenity, and calmness when the world around them was anything but.

As the community and the world relaxed its pandemic response, the medical community at Reliance Hospital heaved a huge sigh of relief. While the pandemic wasn't over and likely wouldn't be for some time, they had weathered the brunt of the storm. Reliance Hospital had survived.

Dr. Greg Hicks wasn't usually keen about attending hospital events, such as award ceremonies. He considered them obligatory, even boring. But as his wife, who was dressed to the nines, straightened his collar for the black-tie event, he found himself looking forward to the night ahead.

It was Reliance's first ABI award ceremony since the pandemic hit, and Phil said he wanted to go all out for this one. The medical professionals and staff at their hospital deserved it.

"This has been the most difficult year in my career at Reliance Hospital," he said into the microphone. "It was unexpected, and we were unprepared. Our weaknesses were exposed, and while we struggled and faltered at times, we managed to pull through our most challenging year with brand integrity. That is why we continually perform brand integrity audits and why we applaud and celebrate those who embody our mission statement as they carry out their duties with our prestigious award, the ABI.

"This year, we will be awarding more ABIs than we have in the past, and I think everyone in this room will agree that every one of them is well deserved," he continued. "Our first ABI is awarded to our entire housekeeping staff, who were called on to maintain a level of sanitation and cleanliness that was unprecedented. We entrusted them with the great responsibility of keeping staff and patients safe, while limiting exposure to the virus to the minimum. They met that responsibility admirably. For work well done under trying circumstances, I award each and every member of the Housekeeping Department with this year's ABI," he said to the applause of the attendees.

Phillip then presented individual ABIs to nearly a dozen more employees, thanking them for their dedication, loyalty, and commitment to brand integrity.

"Now, because Dr. Hicks nominated them, I would like him to present the next ABI awards," he said, inviting Greg to the front of the room.

"In the ED, we have been in a position to get a firsthand glimpse into how the public and our patients have been impacted by the pandemic. However, one employee who was brought to my attention was not in my department at all. She was a nurse I had never met, but I am sure glad I had the opportunity to work with her in a surprising and unexpected way. I encountered Sherry Wells as I was taking a short walk outside, and I witnessed her approach a man who was obviously distraught. Sherry had just gotten off duty after working extra hours, but she didn't hesitate to stop and ask this man if she could help him. That day, I watched a compassionate nurse find a way to help a man witness the birth of his child without being able to enter the building. Because of her, his experience turned from devastating to celebratory, and he experienced a day he will remember for all the right reasons—happy reasons," Greg announced with pride in his voice. "Sherry, you deserve this special award, and I congratulate you for everything you do."

"Next, I'd like to present an ABI award to Christy, a former emergency department nurse. I understand that this is the first time an ABI award will be presented to someone who is no longer employed at Reliance Hospital, but it is well deserved. You see, as I've learned, the Audit of Brand Integrity is meant to show us what we are doing right, but it's also meant to show us when something is out of integrity. That's exactly what Christy did; she illuminated. You see, as an expecting mother, Christy realized that the pandemic put her and her unborn child in an uncomfortable, even fearful position. Rather than pretending and hoping her anguish would go away, she did exactly as we are all taught—find what's wrong, face it, follow it, and fix it, even if that meant resigning from her job. Christy made a difficult decision when she resigned, but she did what was right for her and her child, and in doing so, she did what was right for Reliance

Hospital. As I present her with her ABI, I also invite her to return to Reliance when she's ready. Congratulations to you all."

Last, but not least, Phil took the floor again, this time to present the prestigious Briggs Award of Brand Integrity.

"Walker Briggs embodied everything Reliance is about. He was the spokesperson for our brand, and everyone knew it. He's a tough act to follow, but every year, we manage to find one person who deserves to be the recipient of the honor that bears his name. The winner of this year's BABI, ironically, didn't agree with our pandemic response, at least initially. And he was vocal about it. He complained about the restrictions, the policies, the rules, and the guidelines frequently, but he did so because he cares—he cares about the patients, their families, and the people who work for and with him. I respect him for that.

"However, it was because he cares that he recognized that while we were worried about loss of funding, a lack of supplies, staff shortages, and other issues that we'd never faced, we were overlooking two components of our brand. As Duncan and Vivian would say, the components are so vital that if we failed to find a way to implement them, we would be likely to fall on our own sword and commit what we call brandslaughter. These components are 'the kindest touch' and 'compassionate care.' It is no coincidence that these two components were also the characteristics that Walker embodied every day at Reliance Hospital.

"This year's BABI recipient reminded us that amidst the pandemic and physical distancing guidelines, and with the added stress and angst, we lost our way and were at risk of taking kindness out of our touch and compassion out of our care. For that we owe a debt of gratitude to Dr. Greg Hicks. Not only did he bring the problem to our attention, he faced it head on and was involved in finding the solutions we needed to get back on course and be in brand integrity. It was because of Dr. Hicks that the SmEYEles campaign is now fully activated in every department, and I'm happy to say that it has been well received.

"It was also Dr. Hicks who brought to our attention that stress levels were at unprecedented levels. He formed a committee, and together they found the rejuvenation stations that are strategically placed throughout the hospital for both staff and caregivers. Currently, we have four of them. I'm happy to announce tonight that our charitable foundation has raised funds to purchase two more, placing a rejuvenation station™ in 50 percent of our departments.

"We've struggled, and we have faltered. But thanks to employees and professionals like Dr. Hicks, we not only survived the pandemic, but in doing so, we earned the praise of our community. Day after day, Dr. Hicks has been at the front of the line, and while we haven't agreed one hundred percent on everything, he has represented the hospital's response to the pandemic with utmost brand integrity, delivering the highest quality care with compassion and a kind touch. While we all deserve an award for being survivors, Dr. Hicks deserves this very special one because our brand wouldn't have survived without his leadership. Congratulations, Greg. Walker would be proud—I know I am."

about
DAVID M. CORBIN

David Corbin has been referred to as "Robin Williams with an MBA" because of his very practical, high-content speeches, coupled with entertaining and sometimes side-splitting stories and applications. A former psychotherapist, he has served as a management and leadership consultant to businesses and organizations of all sizes—from Fortune 20 companies to businesses with less than one million—and enjoys the challenges of all. He has worked directly with the offices of the presidents of companies such as AT&T, Hallmark, Sprint, as well as the Hon. Secretary of Veterans Administration and others.

Davidcorbin.com

other books by
DAVID M. CORBIN

Other books authored by David M. Corbin:
https://www.amazon.com/David-M.-
Corbin/e/B0028OJQR4%3Fref=dbs_a_mng_rwt_scns_share

Psyched On Service

From ChangeVictim to ChangeMaster

Illuminate: Harnessing the Positive Power of Negative Thinking

From Internment to Fullfillment (with Neary Heng)

Point Count: From Image to Influence (with Phillip Wexler)

Preventing BrandSlaughter

keynotes

David presents award-winning keynote speeches on each of the books. Contact Melanie@davidcorbin.com

movies

Pass It On (host)
https://www.youtube.com/watch?v=W5708QYshRo

Three Feet From Gold (appearance)

WISHMAN (appearance)

television

The List TV https://www.thelisttv.com/the-list/are-you-killing-your-personal-brand-2-3-21/

The List TV https://www.thelisttv.com/the-list/illuminate-the-negative-8-24-20/